Money Ninja for Teens
A Ninja Life Hacks Guide to Financial Wisdom and Wealth

This book is dedicated to my sons - Mikey, Kobe, and Jojo.

Also by Mary Nhin:

Resilient Ninja | Business Ninja | Emotions Ninja for Teens | Growth Mindset Ninja for Teens | Leadership Ninja for Teens | Self-Management Ninja for Teens | Self-Awareness Ninja for Teens | Social Awareness Ninja for Teens | Decision-MakingNinja for Teens | Relationship Ninja for Teens | Money Ninja for Teens | Angry Ninja | Inventor Ninja | Positive Ninja | Lazy Ninja | Helpful Ninja | Grumpy Ninja | Earth Ninja | Kind Ninja | Perfect Ninja | Anxious Ninja | Money Ninja | Gritty Ninja | Dishonest Ninja | Shy Ninja | Unplugged Ninja | Diversity Ninja | Inclusive Ninja | Masked Ninja | Grateful Ninja | Hangry Ninja | Focused Ninja | Calm Ninja | Brave Ninja | Worry Ninja | Funny Ninja | Patient Ninja | Organized Ninja | Communication Ninja | Stressed Ninja | Smart Ninja | Hopeful Ninja | Confident Ninja | Zen Ninja | Goal-setting | Lonely Ninja | Self-Disciplined Ninja | Motivated Ninja | Sad Ninja | Impulsive Ninja | Feelings Ninja | Creative Ninja | Forgetful Ninja | Nervous Ninja | Emotionally Intelligent Ninja | Growth Mindset Ninja | Jealous Ninja | Frustrated Ninja | Memory Ninja | Listening Ninja | Innovative Ninja | Supportive Ninja | Love Ninja | Humble Ninja | Quiet Ninja | Compassionate Ninja | Sharing Ninja | Caring Ninja | Curious Ninja | Hard-working Ninja | Investments | Problem-Solving Ninja | Integrity Ninja | Disappointed Ninja | eNinja | Healthy Ninja | Adaptable Ninja | Respectful Ninja | Flexible Thinking Ninja | Entrepreneur Ninja | Accountable Ninja | Consent Ninja | Negative Ninja | Sensory Ninja | Tired Ninja | Social Ninja | Neurodivergent Ninja | Happy Ninja | Visionary Ninja | Passionate Ninja | Honest Ninja | Authentic Ninja | Loyal Ninja | Debate Ninja | Collaborative Ninja | Distracted Ninja | Embarrassed Ninja | Negotiator Ninja | Cooperative Ninja | Furious Ninja | Scared Ninja | I Love You, Little Ninja | Gritty Ninja and the St. Patrick's Day Race | Kind Ninja and the Easter Egg Hunt | I Love You, Mom - Earth Ninja | I Love You, Dad - Grumpy Ninja | Patient Ninja's Halloween | Grateful Ninja's Thanksgiving | Ninja Life Hacks Christmas | Ninjas Know the CBT Triangle | Ninjas Go to the Dentist | Ninjas Go to Europe | Ninja Go Camping | Ninjas Go to the Library | Ninjas Go Through a Ninja Warrior Obstacle Course | Ninjas Go to a Party | Ninjas Go to Space | Ninjas Go to Work | Ninjas Go to School | Ninja Life Hacks Numbers | Ninja Life Hacks ABCs of Feelings | Ninja Life Hacks Shapes | Ninja Life Hacks Colors | Ninja Life Hacks Body Parts | Ninja Life Hacks Animals | Ninja Life Hacks Opposites | Ninja Life Hacks Weather | Unplugged Ninja in Vietnam | Kind Ninja Builds a Buddy Bench | Magical Mistake Machine | Lunar New Year | Happy Birthday Ninja | Ninja's New Year | Chef Ninja | Engineer Ninja | Teacher Ninja | Doctor Ninja | Firefighter Ninja | Police Officer Ninja | President Ninja | Coding Ninja | Neurologist Ninja | Amelia Earhart | Steve Jobs | Elon Musk | Indra Nooyi | Anne Frank | Serena Williams | Albert Einstein | Mae Jemison | Frida Kahlo | Michael Jordan | Jane Goodall | Helen Keller | Muhammad Ali | The Wright Brothers | Kobe Bryant | Rosa Parks | Ray Kroc | Martin Luther King, Jr. | Michelle Obama | Sara Blakely | Barack Obama | Walt Disney | Peggy Cherng | David Bowie | Mia Hamm | Sam Walton | Tiger Woods | Jackie Robinson | Mother Teresa | Harriet Tubman | Chloe Kim | Neil Armstrong | Ella Fitzgerald | Stevie Wonder | Maya Angelou | Wilma Rudolph | Lionel Messi | Cristiano Ronaldo | Sophie Cruz | Taylor Swift | Sonia Gandhi | Never Ever Marry a Mermaid | Never Ever Lick a Llama | Never Ever Upset a Unicorn | Never Ever Massage a Moose | Never Ever Dance with Dracula | Never Ever Tickle a Turkey | Never Ever Race a Reindeer

Money Ninja for Teens
A Ninja Life Hacks Guide to Financial Wisdom and Wealth

by Mary Nhin

Money Ninja for Teens: A Ninja Life Hacks Guide to Financial Wisdom and Wealth
© 2025 Mary Nhin | Ninja Life Hacks
All rights reserved.

No part of this book may be reproduced, distributed, or transmitted in any form or by any means, including photocopying, recording, or other electronic or mechanical methods, without the prior written permission of the publisher, except in the case of brief quotations embodied in critical reviews and certain other noncommercial uses permitted by copyright law.

For permission requests, please contact the publisher at:
Grow Grit Press LLC
info@ninjalifehacks.tv

First Edition: 2025
Paperback ISBN: 979-8-89614-085-6
Hardcover ISBN: 979-8-89614-087-0
eBook ISBN: 979-8-89614-086-3

Published by:
Grow Grit Press LLC

ninjalifehacks.tv

Disclaimer: The information provided in this book is based on the author's personal experiences and research. It is intended for educational and informational purposes only. The author and publisher make no guarantees of success or improvement from applying the strategies outlined in this book. Readers are encouraged to consult professionals before making health, financial, legal, or business decisions. Some stories in this book are inspired by real events or composite experiences from friends, students, etc. They're meant to illustrate typical teen challenges.

Printed in the United States of America.

TABLE OF CONTENTS

Author's Note	8
Introduction	9
Part I: INTRODUCTION TO MONEY NINJA	**11**
1. Chapter 1: What is a Money Ninja?	13
2. Chapter 2: Money Mindset	23
3. Chapter 3: Earnings	35
4. Chapter 4: Credit & Debt	43
Part II: SAVE	**59**
5. Chapter 5: Savings	61
6. Chapter 6: Goal-setting	73
Part III: INVEST	**85**
7. Chapter 7: Investments	87
8. Chapter 8: Entrepreneurship	101
Part IV: DONATE	**113**
9. Chapter 9: Generosity	115
Part V: CONCLUSION TO MONEY NINJA	**125**
10. Chapter 10: Protect Your Money Like a Ninja	127
11. Chapter 11: Money Pitfalls Ninjas Can Avoid	137
12. Chapter 12: Your Money Future	147
Final Thoughts	156
Money Ninja Glossary	158
Money Ninja Challenges	160
About the Author	169

AUTHOR'S NOTE

Dear Reader,

When I was a teenager, no one really taught me about money. I learned the hard way, through trial and error, missed opportunities, and some pretty embarrassing financial mistakes. That's why I wrote Money Ninja for Teens, to give you the money wisdom I wish I had back then.

This book isn't about becoming a millionaire overnight. It's about becoming confident, capable, and in control of your financial future. Whether you dream of owning your own business, buying your first car, or simply feeling less stressed about money, this book is your guide.

You don't have to be an adult to start making smart money moves. In fact, the earlier you start, the more freedom and choices you'll have down the road. So whether you're earning your first paycheck or just saving birthday money, you're already ahead of the game by picking up this book.

Let's get started.
– Mary Nhin

INTRODUCTION

Welcome to *Money Ninja for Teens*, your crash course in how to earn, save, invest, and grow your money like a boss.

Money might seem complicated, but the truth is, it's just a tool. And like any tool, once you learn how to use it, you can build something amazing. You can create your dream life, help the people you love, and never feel stuck in a job you hate just to pay the bills.

This book is packed with real-life stories, expert advice, and simple strategies that actually work, no boring lectures here. You'll learn the difference between needs and wants, how to avoid debt traps, how to spot a scam, and how to start investing, even as a teen.

And don't worry, we'll make it fun. There are quizzes, journal reflections, action challenges, and thought bubbles to keep you thinking, growing, and making moves like a true Money Ninja.

Ready to unlock the secret to financial freedom? Let's do this.

PART I

INTRODUCTION TO MONEY NINJA

1

WHAT IS A MONEY NINJA?

The Secret to Financial Success

Money is more than just something you use to buy things, it's a tool that can give you freedom. Freedom to make choices, freedom to follow your dreams, and freedom to spend your time doing what matters most to you. But here's the catch: most people don't learn how to manage money until they've already made mistakes. That's why becoming a Money Ninja early is so important.

Money = Freedom

When you have money, you have the ability to choose how you live your life instead of having your circumstances decide for you. Here's how money can give you different types of freedom:

1. Financial Freedom – You're not constantly stressed about money, and you can cover your needs without worrying about every dollar.
2. Freedom to Choose – You have the power to make decisions based on what's best for you, not just what's cheapest or most convenient.

3. Freedom of Time – Instead of working paycheck to paycheck in a job you don't like, financial security lets you spend time doing things that truly matter to you.

Think about it: Would you rather work at a job just to pay the bills, or have enough financial security to do work you love? Would you rather be stuck in a situation you don't like because you can't afford to leave, or have enough savings to walk away and build something better?

Money itself isn't the goal, freedom is the goal. And smart money management is the key to achieving that freedom.

The New Definition of Success

Money isn't just paper or numbers in a bank account, it's a tool. And like any tool, it's only useful if you know how to use it wisely. The real power of money isn't in buying more things; it's in creating opportunities for yourself and others.

A Money Ninja understands that money isn't the goal, it's a way to build the life you want. Here's how money can work for you:

- It Gives You Choices – Instead of being stuck doing something you don't enjoy, money allows you to choose where you live, what you do, and who you spend time with.
- It Buys You Time – Instead of trading every hour for a paycheck, smart money management helps you free up time to focus on your passions.
- It Creates Opportunities – Education, travel, starting a business, having money can open doors that might otherwise be closed.
- It Helps You Help Others – True success isn't just about what you have, it's about what you give. Money allows you to make a difference in your family, community, and even the world.

A lot of people chase money because they think it will bring them happiness. But being wealthy isn't just about the size of your bank account, it's about having control over your time, your choices, and your impact on the world.

Success today isn't just about making money, it's about using money to create freedom, fulfillment, and purpose. A Money Ninja knows that true wealth is measured in more than just dollars.

Importance of a Hard Work Ethic and Being Smart With Money

Some people think success is just about getting lucky or making the right investments, but nothing replaces hard work. Even the richest and most successful people put in the work and hustle:

- Athletes train for years before they win championships.
- Entrepreneurs fail multiple times before they build a great business.
- Artists and musicians spend hours perfecting their craft before they make it big.

The key is combining hard work with smart money habits. If you learn how to earn, save, and invest wisely while working toward your goals, you're setting yourself up for long-term success.

Hard work gets you started, but working smart keeps you ahead. Money Ninjas don't just grind, they find ways to make their money work for them. That's why it's important to learn skills like:

- Budgeting so you're in control of your money.
- Investing so your money grows while you sleep.
- Entrepreneurship so you can create your own opportunities.

The real flex isn't just making money, it's having the freedom to do what you love while making an impact. That's the new success.

What Makes a Money Ninja Different?

Being a Money Ninja isn't about being rich, it's about being smart with your money. When you understand how to earn, save, invest, and spend wisely, you set yourself up for a future where you're in control, not just reacting to financial stress. True wealth isn't just about how much money you have; it's about how well you use it.

Most people think money is just for spending, but a Money Ninja knows there are three powerful ways to use money:

1. Save – Put money aside for future goals and unexpected expenses.
2. Invest – Grow your money over time by making smart financial choices.
3. Donate – Use money to help others and make an impact in your community.

By balancing these three areas, you'll build a financial foundation that allows you to live life on your own terms.

You might be thinking, "Why do I need to worry about money now? I'm just a teenager." The truth is, the earlier you start learning about money, the better off you'll be. Money habits start forming young, and the choices you make now can set you up for success (or struggle) later.

Imagine being able to buy your first car, travel to new places, or even start your own business, all because you learned to be a Money Ninja early on. Financial literacy isn't just about numbers, it's about having the power to create the life you want.

Expert Advice

"The way to get started is to quit talking and begin doing." , Walt Disney

A Money Ninja doesn't just talk about goals, they take action. Your financial journey begins the moment you decide to take control.

Actionable Strategies

- Save – Put money aside for future goals and unexpected expenses.

- Invest – Grow your money over time by making smart financial choices.
- Donate – Use money to help others and make an impact in your community.

"**Financial** freedom is available to those who learn about it and work for it."
– ROBERT KIYOSAKI

Personal Story: My First Money Lesson

When I was a teenager, I wanted the latest sneakers. Everyone at school had them, and I felt like I needed them too. My parents told me that if I really wanted them, I'd have to buy them with my own money. So, I saved up my birthday cash, did extra chores, and finally had enough to buy them.

At first, I felt unstoppable, until I realized I had spent all my money. The next week, my friends invited me to a movie, but I had nothing left to spend. That's when I learned my first big money lesson: spending everything now means having nothing later. From that day on, I made sure to always keep some money saved so I wouldn't be stuck in that situation again.

This is why learning to be a Money Ninja early matters. The choices you make with money now will impact your freedom later.

Quick Quiz Box

True or False:

1. Money is only for spending.
2. Financial freedom means never having to think about money.
3. Saving money now can give you more choices in the future.

(Answers: F, F, T)

Journal Reflection Box

Write about a time you had to make a decision about money. Did you save, spend, or give? Would you do anything differently now?

Action Challenge Chart

Task	Goal	Outcome
Save $5 this week	Start small savings habit	Learned to set aside money
Track spending for 7 days	See where money goes	Became aware of spending habits
Set a mini money goal	Save for something meaningful	Developed goal-setting skills

Mini-FAQ: Money Ninja Questions

Q1: What's the first step to becoming a Money Ninja?
A: Start by setting a small money goal, saving $10, tracking expenses, or avoiding impulse buys for a week.

Q2: Is being a Money Ninja about being rich?
A: Nope! It's about being in control of your money so you have more freedom in life.

Q3: Why should I care about this now?
A: The sooner you learn about money, the fewer mistakes you'll make later, and the more freedom you'll have!

> **Money Ninja Takeaway**
>
> Anyone can become a Money Ninja if they choose to learn and grow.

2

MONEY MINDSET

Why Your Mindset Matters

Your mindset about money is just as important as how much you have. If you believe that money is hard to earn, impossible to manage, or only for "rich people," you're already setting yourself up for financial struggles. A Money Ninja understands that money is a skill, not just luck, and anyone can develop that skill.

Your thoughts and beliefs about money affect how you handle it. If you see money as something you control, you'll make smarter decisions. But if you think money controls you, it's easy to feel stuck.

Here's how a Money Ninja thinks differently:

Old Mindset: "I'm too young to save."

Money Ninja Mindset: "The earlier I start, the better my future will be."

Old Mindset: "Money is complicated."

Money Ninja Mindset: "Money is a skill I can learn."

Old Mindset: "Only rich people have money."

Money Ninja Mindset: "Wealth is built by good habits, not just luck."

Many people grow up hearing negative messages about money, like "Money is the root of all evil" or "You have to work too hard to ever get ahead." The problem? These beliefs hold you back from making smart financial choices.

How to Develop a Money Ninja Mindset

To change your money mindset, start questioning these beliefs:

Where did I learn this belief?

Is it true, or just something I heard?

What's a better way to think about money?

For example, instead of thinking, "I'll never be good with money," try saying, "I can learn new money skills just like anything else."

Your mindset affects your habits, and your habits shape your financial future. The way you think about money influences the choices you make every day, and those choices add up over time. If you want to build wealth and financial security, it all starts with developing a strong money mindset.

One of the best habits you can develop is saving money early, even if it's just a few dollars a week. Small amounts may not seem like much, but over time, they add up. The earlier you start saving, the more opportunities you have to grow your money through smart decisions.

Another important step is to pay attention to where your money goes. Many people have no idea how much they're actually spending each month. Tracking your expenses, even for just a week, can open your eyes to spending habits you didn't even realize you had. The more awareness you have, the better choices you can make.

Setting small financial goals can also help you build momentum. Whether it's saving up for something special, paying off a small debt, or reaching a certain amount in your bank account, celebrating these milestones keeps you motivated. Achieving small goals makes bigger financial goals feel more possible.

It's also important to educate yourself about money. Financial literacy isn't something most schools teach, so it's up to you to seek out knowledge. Reading books, listening to podcasts, and learning from financially successful people can give you insights that will help you avoid common money mistakes and build wealth the right way.

One of the biggest money lessons comes from Robert Kiyosaki's book Rich Dad Poor Dad: Understanding the difference between assets and liabilities. This concept is key to becoming financially independent.

Understanding the difference between assets and liabilities is one of the most important financial lessons you can learn. It's what separates those who build wealth from those who struggle financially. Many people work hard to earn money, but if they keep spending it on liabilities instead of investing in assets, they'll always feel like they're stuck in the same place. A Money Ninja knows that the key to financial freedom is accumulating assets that generate income over time.

What Are Assets?

Assets are things that put money into your pocket. They grow in value, provide passive income, or contribute to your financial security. Think of assets as tools that work for you, even while you sleep. The more assets you have, the less you have to rely on just earning a paycheck to survive.

Examples of assets include:

- Investments – Stocks, bonds, and mutual funds that grow in value over time.

- Savings – Money saved in high-interest accounts that earns interest over time.
- Businesses – A business you own (even a small side hustle) that generates income.
- Real Estate – Rental properties that earn money from tenants or homes that increase in value.
- Intellectual Property – Books, courses, patents, or music that generate royalties.

If you focus on acquiring assets, your money begins working for you instead of you constantly working for money. This is why wealthy people invest their earnings instead of just spending them, they understand that money should be used to create more money.

What Are Liabilities?

Liabilities are things that take money out of your pocket. They don't help you build wealth; instead, they drain your finances and can make it harder to get ahead. Some liabilities are necessary, like rent or transportation, but too many liabilities, especially bad debt, can keep you financially trapped.

Examples of liabilities include:

- Credit Card Debt – Borrowing money at high interest rates can quickly spiral out of control.
- Car Loans – A car loses value over time, and the monthly payments take money from your income.
- Student Loans – Education can be valuable, but debt must be managed wisely to avoid financial stress.
- Unnecessary Luxury Items – Expensive clothes, electronics, or gadgets that don't provide long-term value.

Many people mistakenly believe that things like cars and big houses are assets because they seem valuable. But unless they generate income or increase in value over time, they are actually liabilities. A Money Ninja understands that just because something looks impressive, it doesn't mean it's making them richer.

The Secret to Wealth

The goal is not to avoid all liabilities, but to make sure your assets grow faster than your liabilities. If you build enough assets, you can eventually afford the things you want without financial stress.

For example, instead of buying a fancy car right away, a Money Ninja might invest in stocks or start a small business. If that business eventually earns enough money to pay for the car, then they've turned an asset into a way to fund a liability, without going into debt. This is the kind of smart money move that leads to long-term financial success.

If you want to build wealth, ask yourself this question before making a financial decision:

"Is this putting money into my pocket, or taking money out?"

If it's an asset, it's helping you grow financially. If it's a liability, you need to think carefully before spending. The more you focus on accumulating assets and limiting unnecessary liabilities, the closer you'll get to financial freedom.

A Money Ninja doesn't just work for money, they make money work for them. Would you rather spend your life paying for things that lose value, or own things that create more opportunities? The choice is yours.

A Money Ninja focuses on building assets instead of just spending money on liabilities. The goal is to make money work for you rather than constantly working for money. By developing the right mindset, making smart choices, and learning how to grow your wealth, you can set yourself up for financial success and freedom.

The Foundation of Financial Freedom

At its core, money management comes down to two simple things: how much money you bring in (income) and how much money goes out (expenses). Mastering this balance is the key to financial success. If your income is always higher than your expenses, you'll have the ability to save, invest, and build wealth. If your expenses constantly drain your income, you'll always be struggling to keep up.

Income is the money you earn, and it can come from multiple sources. Many people rely only on a paycheck from their job, but a Money Ninja understands the power of multiple income streams, finding different ways to earn money so they are never dependent on just one source.

Some common types of income include:

- Earned Income – Money you make from working a job, whether hourly, salaried, or freelance.
- Business Income – Money earned from a business you own, such as selling products or services.
- Passive Income – Money that keeps coming in with little ongoing effort, such as rental income, dividends, or royalties from books and music.
- Investment Income – Earnings from investments like stocks, bonds, or real estate.
- Side Hustle Income – Extra money from part-time work, gigs, or online businesses.

A Money Ninja doesn't just rely on a single paycheck, they look for ways to create multiple streams of income. That way, if one source of money slows down, they still have others to rely on.

Expenses are the things you spend money on, and they fall into two main categories: needs and wants.

- Needs are essentials, things you must pay for to survive, such as food, housing, and utilities.
- Wants are things that bring enjoyment but aren't necessary, such as eating out, entertainment, and new clothes.

It's important to understand that some expenses can be fixed (they stay the same each month, like rent or car payments) while others are variable (they change from month to month, like groceries or entertainment).

The Key to Financial Success

One of the biggest financial mistakes people make is letting their expenses grow every time their income increases. This is called lifestyle inflation, as soon as you make more money, you start spending more on nicer things, like a fancier car, expensive clothes, or eating out more often.

A Money Ninja avoids this trap by keeping their expenses low while increasing their income. That way, they have more money left over to save, invest, and build wealth. Instead of spending all of a raise or bonus, they use a portion of it to buy assets that will generate even more income in the future.

If you want to gain financial freedom, your income should always be greater than your expenses. Here's how to make that happen:

1. Increase Your Income – Look for new ways to earn money, whether through a side hustle, learning new skills, investing, or starting a business.
2. Lower Your Expenses – Cut unnecessary spending, find ways to save on essential costs, and avoid impulse purchases.
3. Track Your Money – Pay attention to where every dollar goes. A Money Ninja never lets their money disappear without knowing where it went.
4. Live Below Your Means – Just because you can afford something doesn't mean you should buy it. Make smart spending choices and focus on the long-term benefits.
5. Use Extra Money Wisely – Instead of wasting extra income on things that lose value, put it toward assets that will grow your wealth.

A Money Ninja doesn't just work hard to make money, they also work smart to keep it. Every financial decision should have a purpose, whether it's saving for a goal, investing in future income, or enjoying life without financial stress.

If you control your expenses and grow your income wisely, you won't have to worry about money running out. Instead, you'll be in charge of your finances, and that's the ultimate financial freedom.

Expert Advice

"Whether you think you can or think you can't, you're right."
— Henry Ford

Your mindset shapes your money habits. Believing in yourself is the first investment that pays off.

Actionable Strategies

- Challenge your money beliefs – Write down three thoughts you have about money. Are they helping you or holding you back?
- Start a money habit today – Save $1 a day, track your spending, or set a small financial goal.
- Think like a Money Ninja – Whenever you make a money decision, ask yourself: "Is this helping me or hurting my financial future?"

"The secret to wealth is simple: Find a way to do more for others than anyone else does."
– TONY ROBBINS

Personal Story: The Time I Thought Money Didn't Matter

When I was younger, I thought money wasn't something I needed to think about. My parents paid for everything, so why should I care? That changed when I wanted my own phone. My parents said if I wanted one, I had to pay for the bill myself.

At first, I thought it was unfair. But then I started saving money from chores and small jobs. The first time I paid my own bill, I felt independent. I wasn't just spending money, I was managing it. That's when I realized: money isn't about things, it's about responsibility and freedom.

Quick Quiz Box

True or False:

1. Your mindset affects how you handle money.
2. You have to be rich to become good with money.
3. Small money habits don't make a difference.

(*Answers: T, F, F*)

Journal Reflection Box

What is one belief you have about money? Where did it come from? Does it help or hold you back?

Action Challenge Chart

Task	Goal	Outcome
Write down 3 money beliefs	Identify limiting beliefs	Learn how mindset affects money
Save $1 a day for a week	Build saving habits	See small savings add up
Track spending for 7 days	Become aware of spending habits	Make smarter financial choices

Mini-FAQ: Money Mindset Questions

Q1: Can I really change my money mindset?
A: Absolutely! Just like learning any skill, you can rewire your thinking and create better money habits.

Q2: Does thinking positively about money mean I'll get rich?
A: No, but it helps you make smarter choices that lead to financial success.

Q3: What's the easiest way to start improving my money mindset?
A: Pay attention to how you talk about money. Replace negative thoughts with empowering ones!

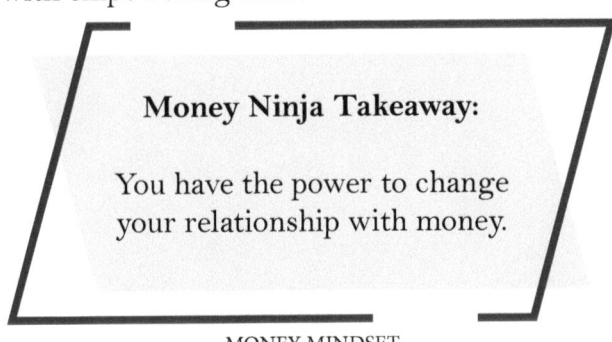

Money Ninja Takeaway:

You have the power to change your relationship with money.

3

EARNINGS

The First Step to Financial Freedom

Money doesn't just appear, you have to earn it. But not all income is the same. A Money Ninja understands that the key to financial freedom isn't just working hard, it's making money work for you.

There are two main ways to make money: earned income and passive income. Earned income is the money you work for, such as wages from a job, gig work, freelance projects, or even an allowance. Passive income, on the other hand, is money that works for you. This includes earnings from investments, royalties, rental properties, or online businesses that generate income even when you're not actively working.

Most people rely solely on earned income, which means they must trade their time for money. The problem with this approach is that there are only so many hours in a day, and eventually, you'll hit a limit on how much you can earn. A Money Ninja thinks differently. Instead of depending on a single source of income, they build multiple income streams so that money continues to flow in, even while they sleep.

Earning money isn't just about making cash, it's about doing it responsibly. The type of work you choose matters. A Money

Ninja looks for opportunities that align with their values, rather than simply chasing the highest-paying gig. They also balance work with school, family, and personal time to avoid burnout. And most importantly, they don't just spend everything they earn; they save, invest, and grow their money wisely.

If you're wondering where to start, there are plenty of side hustles and jobs that teens can do right now. Some options provide flexible, work-from-home opportunities, while others offer steady paychecks and valuable experience.

If you prefer flexible work you can do from anywhere, consider launching a side hustle. You could sell handmade products on Etsy, tutor younger students, babysit or pet sit, create and sell digital art or printables, manage social media accounts for small businesses, or resell clothes and sneakers online. These side hustles allow you to earn money on your own schedule while developing valuable skills.

If you'd rather have a part-time job with a steady paycheck, consider working at a local store, coffee shop, or restaurant. You could also coach kids' sports teams, lifeguard at a community pool, teach music or dance lessons, or even freelance on platforms like Fiverr or Upwork. These jobs not only provide reliable income but also teach discipline, time management, and customer service skills that will be useful in any career.

Inspiring Young Entrepreneurs Who Started Early

Some teens have even taken small ideas and turned them into major businesses. Moziah Bridges, for example, started designing bow ties at just nine years old and now runs a successful fashion brand called Mo's Bows. Mikaila Ulmercreated a lemonade brand, Me & the Bees Lemonade, and donates part of her profits to bee conservation. Ryan Kajibegan reviewing toys on YouTube and grew his Ryan's World channel into a multimillion-dollar brand.

What do these young entrepreneurs have in common? They didn't wait for the "right time", they took action. They found creative ways to earn money while doing something they loved. If they can do it, so can you. The first step is simply getting started.

Two Main Ways to Make Money

1. Earned Income – Money you work for (jobs, gigs, freelance work, or allowance).
2. Passive Income – Money that works for you (investments, royalties, rental income, or online businesses).

Expert Advice

"Do not save what is left after spending, but spend what is left after saving." — Warren Buffett

Be intentional with your money, plan your spending after you've saved, not the other way around.

Actionable Strategies

- Pick one side hustle to try – Start small and experiment with a way to earn money that excites you.
- Set an earning goal – Decide how much money you want to make in a month and track your progress.
- Think long-term – Instead of just earning money to spend, plan how you can reinvest it to grow your wealth.

"**Never** depend on a single income. Make investment to create a second source."
– WARREN BUFFETT

Personal Story: My First Side Hustle

When I was younger, I wanted to make extra money, but I didn't want a regular job. So, I started offering to wash cars in my neighborhood. At first, I only had one or two customers, but after a few weeks, word spread, and I had regular clients.

I learned a few things quickly:

1. Good service brings repeat customers – People liked my work, so they kept coming back.
2. Earning money felt amazing – I wasn't just relying on an allowance, I had control over my own money.
3. I could expand – Eventually, I asked a friend to help, and we made even more!

That first side hustle showed me that earning money isn't just about working hard, it's about working smart.

Quick Quiz Box

True or False:

1. You should rely on just one source of income.
2. Passive income means you don't have to work at all.
3. Teen entrepreneurs can be successful.

(Answers: F, F, T)

Journal Reflection Box

What kind of work excites you the most? Do you prefer a steady job or starting your own business?

Action Challenge Chart

Task	Goal	Outcome
Choose a side hustle	Start earning extra money	Gained financial independence
Set an income goal	Track progress	Learned goal-setting skills
Try one passive income idea	Make money work for you	Built long-term financial habits

Mini-FAQ: Earnings Questions

Q1: What's the best way for a teen to start earning money?
A: Find something you enjoy that people are willing to pay for, whether it's babysitting, selling art, or tutoring.

Q2: Do I need a business to start earning money?
A: No! You can start with part-time jobs, side gigs, or freelance work before launching a full business.

Q3: Why should I care about multiple income streams?
A: The more ways you earn, the more financial security and freedom you'll have!

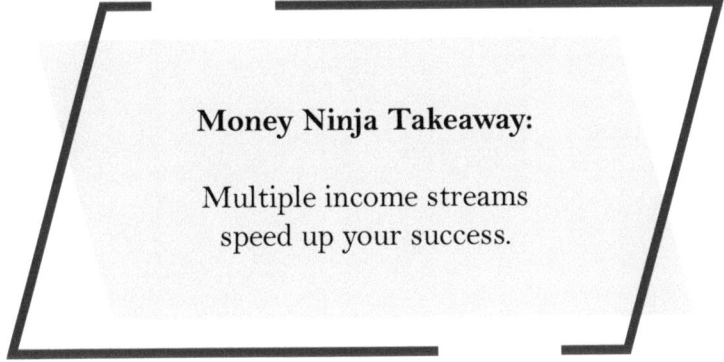

Money Ninja Takeaway:

Multiple income streams speed up your success.

4

CREDIT & DEBT

Using Credit

A Money Ninja knows that credit is a tool, not free money. Used wisely, it can help you build a strong financial future. Used carelessly, it can lead to financial stress.

Understanding credit and debt is an important part of becoming financially independent.

Debt is money that you borrow with the agreement to pay it back later, usually with interest. Common types of debt include:

- Credit Cards – Borrow money to make purchases, with the option to pay it off over time.
- Student Loans – Money borrowed for education, which must be paid back after graduation.
- Auto Loans & Mortgages – Loans used to buy a car or house, paid back in monthly installments.

A Money Ninja understands that not all debt is bad, but borrowing more than you can afford can create long-term financial problems.

Not all debt is created equal. Some debt helps you grow financially, while other debt can hold you back.

Good Debt: Student loans (if used wisely), mortgages, business loans (when investing in a profitable idea).

Bad Debt: High-interest credit cards, payday loans, buying unnecessary items with borrowed money.

A Money Ninja only takes on debt when necessary and when it provides long-term value.

Understanding Debt and Compound Interest: The Double-Edged Sword

Debt can either work for you or work against you, it all depends on how you manage it. While some types of debt, like student loans or mortgages, can be considered investments in your future, other kinds, especially credit card debt, can quickly spiral out of control. A Money Ninja knows how to use debt wisely and avoid the trap of paying more than they borrow.

One of the most dangerous aspects of debt is compound interest, which can work in your favor when you're investing but can also work against you when you owe money. If you don't understand how interest works, you could end up paying far more than you ever borrowed in the first place.

Interest is the cost of borrowing money. When you take out a loan or use a credit card, the lender charges interest as a fee for letting you use their money. The interest rate is the percentage of the loan you must pay back in addition to the amount borrowed.

- What it's based on: Your credit score, loan type, and the lender's policies.
- What the prime rate means: The lowest interest rate banks offer to their best customers. Your rate is usually higher unless you have excellent credit.

A Money Ninja understands that the higher the interest rate, the more money you owe over time.

Compound interest is when interest is charged on both the original amount borrowed (the principal) and the interest that keeps accumulating over time. This means that if you don't pay off your debt quickly, the amount you owe can grow faster than you expect, making it much harder to pay off.

For example, let's say you owe $1,000 on a credit card with an interest rate of 20% per year. If you only make the minimum payment, the unpaid balance continues to grow because you're also paying interest on the interest that was added each month.

Here's how the debt can snowball:

- Month 1: You owe $1,000
- Month 2: Interest adds $16.67, making it $1,016.67
- Month 3: Interest adds $16.94, making it $1,033.61
- By the end of the year, you could owe over $1,200, even if you haven't borrowed more money!

If you only make the minimum payment, it could take years to pay off that $1,000, and you could end up paying double or even triple the original amount.

Buy Now, Pay Later (BNPL) Services (Afterpay, Klarna, etc.)

Many stores now offer BNPL services like Afterpay, Klarna, and Affirm, which let you split a purchase into multiple payments. While this may seem like a great deal, these services can lead to overspending. If you miss a payment, they may charge fees and report it to credit agencies, hurting your credit score.

A Money Ninja asks: Do I really need this, or is this just an excuse to spend more?

Credit Card Danger

Credit cards can be a useful tool, but they can also be a trap. Many people only pay the minimum payment, which leads to long-term debt due to high interest rates. If you don't pay off your balance in full each month, your debt can quickly grow.

Example: If you owe $1,000 on a credit card with a 20% interest rate and only make minimum payments, it could take years to pay off, and you'd end up paying hundreds of dollars in extra interest.

A Money Ninja always pays off their credit card balance in full each month to avoid paying interest.

Used wisely, credit cards can help build your credit score and even earn rewards. Here's how:

1. Set up autopay – Link your credit card to your checking account to pay off the balance every month automatically.
2. Use it for regular expenses – Things like gas, groceries, and bills that you'd pay anyway.
3. Take advantage of cash back – Many credit cards offer 1-2% cash back on purchases, meaning you actually earn money when you use them responsibly.

Your credit score is a number that shows lenders how trustworthy you are with money. A high score makes it easier to get loans, rent apartments, and even get jobs.

Ways to build a strong credit score:

- Pay bills on time – Late payments lower your score.
- Use less than 30% of your available credit – If you have a $1,000 credit limit, try not to borrow more than $300 at a time.
- Keep accounts open – The longer your credit history, the better your score.

A Money Ninja treats credit like trust, something to be earned and protected.

The Snowball Effect of Debt

Debt has a way of growing like a snowball rolling down a hill, the longer it goes unpaid, the bigger it gets. Many people think they can handle small amounts of debt, but when they take on multiple credit cards, student loans, and car payments, it can quickly become overwhelming.

For example, let's say you have:

- $3,000 in credit card debt at 22% interest
- A $5,000 car loan at 8% interest
- A $10,000 student loan at 5% interest

If you only make the minimum payments on all of these, your total debt could double over time due to interest charges. This is why paying off debt as fast as possible is so important.

A Money Ninja understands that debt is not free money, it's borrowing from your future. Here are some key strategies to avoid falling into the debt trap:

- Only use credit if you can pay it off in full each month. This prevents interest from accumulating.
- If you must borrow money, make a plan to pay it off quickly. The faster you pay it off, the less interest you'll owe.
- Avoid only making the minimum payment. It may seem like an easy way to manage debt, but it keeps you stuck in the cycle.
- Live below your means. Just because you qualify for a big loan doesn't mean you should take it.
- Save an emergency fund. Many people go into debt because of unexpected expenses. Having savings can prevent this.

Use Interest to Your Advantage

Instead of paying interest on debt, a Money Ninja flips the script and earns interest by investing in assets that grow over time. Compound interest can be a powerful tool if you're the one collecting it instead of paying it.

Imagine if instead of paying 20% interest on credit card debt, you were earning 8% interest on investments. Over time, your money would grow instead of shrink. The goal is to make money work for you, not the other way around.

A Money Ninja avoids bad debt, pays off balances quickly, and builds wealth by being smart with money. The best way to avoid financial stress in the future is to make smart choices now. Would you rather spend years paying off past purchases, or have the freedom to use your money for things that truly matter? The choice is yours.

Using Credit Cards Wisely

Credit cards can either be a powerful tool or a dangerous trap, it all depends on how you use them. A Money Ninja knows how to make credit cards work for them instead of falling into debt. One of the smartest ways to do this is by taking advantage of cash rebates, rewards, and benefits that certain credit cards offer.

When used responsibly, a good credit card can:

- Earn cash back on everyday purchases
- Help you build a strong credit history
- Provide travel perks, fraud protection, and extended warranties
- Offer rewards that help you save money on things you'd buy anyway

However, the key to winning the credit card game is to always pay your balance in full every month. If you carry a balance and pay interest, those rewards aren't worth it, the interest will cost you more than the cashback you earn.

The Citi® Double Cash Card: A Money Ninja Favorite

One of the best cash-back credit cards for responsible spenders is the Citi® Double Cash Card, which offers a simple and effective way to earn money on your purchases.

- How It Works: You earn 2% cash back on everything you buy, 1% when you make a purchase and another 1% when you pay it off.

- Why It's Great: Unlike some cards that limit rewards to certain categories, this card gives you cash back on every purchase with no special spending rules.
- Annual Fee: $0, so all your rewards are pure profit.

If you're someone who pays off your balance in full every month, this card allows you to earn cash back on everything without having to track categories or worry about rotating bonus rewards.

How to Use a Credit Card Like a Money Ninja

Having a great credit card is only useful if you use it correctly. Here's how a Money Ninja maximizes rewards without getting into debt:

1. Always Pay in Full – Never carry a balance. If you pay in full each month, you avoid interest while still earning rewards.
2. Use Your Card for Everyday Expenses – Instead of paying with cash or a debit card, use your credit card for things you already buy (groceries, gas, bills) to earn cash back on every dollar.
3. Set Up Automatic Payments – This ensures you never miss a due date, helping you avoid late fees and build good credit.
4. Don't Overspend Just for Rewards – Spending an extra $500 to earn $10 in rewards is not worth it if you don't need the items.
5. Take Advantage of Sign-Up Bonuses – Many credit cards offer bonus cash rewards if you spend a certain amount in the first few months. If you already have big purchases planned, use the card to earn free money.
6. Keep Your Credit Utilization Low – Never use more than 30% of your credit limit at a time. If your limit is $1,000, keep your balance below $300 before paying it off.
7. Check Your Credit Score Regularly – Use free services like Credit Karma or Experian to monitor your score and make sure you're building good credit over time.

A Money Ninja doesn't let credit cards control them, they control the credit cards. Used wisely, a good cashback card can earn you free money on the things you already buy while helping you build a strong credit history. But if you fall into the trap of spending beyond your means and paying interest, those rewards won't be worth it.

If you can pay off your balance in full, keep spending under control, and maximize rewards, you'll be able to make money instead of losing it, and that's how a Money Ninja plays the game.

How to Build Credit as a Teen

Building credit as a teenager might not seem important now, but having good credit can open doors for you in the future. A strong credit score helps when applying for an apartment, getting a car loan, or even landing a job. The earlier you start building credit, the easier it will be to qualify for lower interest rates and better financial opportunities later in life. Here are some smart ways to start building credit as a teen:

1. Become an Authorized User on a Parent's Credit Card

One of the easiest ways to start building credit is to ask a parent or guardian to add you as an authorized user on their credit card. This means their credit history for that card will also appear on your credit report. If they have a good payment history, it can help you build positive credit before you even get your own card. However, it's important that they pay their bills on time, because if they miss payments, it can also affect your credit score.

2. Open a Student or Secured Credit Card

Once you turn 18, you may qualify for a student credit card or a secured credit card.
- Student Credit Cards: These are designed for young adults with little or no credit history. They often have lower credit

limits but can help establish a credit record when used responsibly.
- Secured Credit Cards: These require a security deposit (typically $200-$500) that acts as your credit limit. As you use the card and make payments, it builds your credit, and eventually, you may qualify for a traditional (unsecured) credit card.

3. Get a Credit Builder Loan

A credit builder loan is specifically designed to help you build credit. Instead of getting the money upfront, the lender holds the funds in an account while you make small monthly payments. Once you've paid off the loan, you receive the money, and your positive payment history is reported to the credit bureaus. This helps establish a track record of responsible borrowing.

4. Pay Bills in Your Name

Some utility companies, phone carriers, and streaming services allow teens to have bills in their name. If possible, have a cell phone bill, utility bill, or subscription service (like Netflix or Spotify) listed under your name and make sure it's paid on time. Some services report payments to credit bureaus, which helps build credit history.

5. Use a Debit Card Wisely (But Know It Doesn't Build Credit)

While a debit card doesn't directly impact your credit score, learning to manage a checking account and avoid overdrafts can help build responsible financial habits. Some banks offer debit cards that allow you to upgrade to a credit card later, making it a great first step toward credit management.

6. Pay Your Bills on Time, Every Time

Your payment history is the biggest factor in your credit score, making up about 35% of it. Whether it's a credit card, student loan, or phone bill, always pay on time. Even one late payment can hurt your credit score, so setting up automatic payments or reminders is a smart move.

7. Keep Your Credit Utilization Low

Credit utilization refers to how much of your available credit you use. If you have a $500 credit limit and spend $450, your utilization rate is 90%, which can lower your credit score. Try to keep your credit usage below 30% of your limit, meaning if your limit is $500, don't spend more than $150 before paying it off.

8. Avoid Unnecessary Debt

Just because you have a credit card doesn't mean you should max it out. Debt is easy to get into but hard to get out of. Only charge what you can afford to pay off each month, and avoid carrying a balance whenever possible. Paying off your credit card in full each month helps you avoid interest charges and builds a positive credit history.

9. Check Your Credit Score and Report Regularly

Even as a teen, you can check your credit score using free services like Credit Karma, Experian, or AnnualCreditReport.com. Keeping an eye on your credit report helps you spot errors, track your progress, and learn how different actions affect your credit score.

10. Start Saving for Big Purchases Instead of Borrowing

While building credit is important, it's even more important to develop strong financial habits. Instead of relying on credit for big purchases, practice saving first. When you eventually need to finance something like a car or a home, you'll have both a good credit score and solid savings to make smart financial decisions.

    A Money Ninja knows that credit is a tool, it can either help you or hurt you depending on how you use it. By starting early, keeping debt low, and making payments on time, you'll set yourself up for a strong financial future. The key is to use credit wisely so that when you really need it, you'll have a great credit history working in your favor.

Expert Advice

"A budget is telling your money where to go instead of wondering where it went." — John C. Maxwell

Budgets aren't about restriction, they're about control. You're the boss of your money, not the other way around.

Actionable Strategies

- Learn the basics of credit scores – Watch a short video or read a teen-friendly article to understand how credit is built and why it matters.
- Use debit before credit – Practice spending your own money first so you build good habits before taking on debt.
- Set a "borrow-with-a-plan" rule – Only borrow money (or use credit) if you already know how you'll pay it back.
- Track any money you owe – Whether it's $5 to a friend or $50 from a school expense, write it down and pay it off quickly.
- Talk to a parent or mentor about how they manage credit – Ask what they wish they had done differently when they were your age.

"The man who never has enough money to pay his debts has too much of something else."
— JAMES LENDALL BASFORD

How Alex Built Credit as a Teen

Alex was 16 when he first started thinking about his financial future. He knew that one day he would want to rent an apartment, buy a car, and maybe even start a business, but he had no credit history. Instead of waiting until he was older and struggling to get approved for loans, Alex decided to start building credit early.

First, Alex asked his mom to add him as an authorized user on her credit card. She had a good credit score and always paid her balance in full, so every time she used her card responsibly, it helped build Alex's credit history. Even though he didn't use the card much himself, just having his name on the account gave him a credit boost.

When Alex turned 18, he applied for a secured credit card with a $300 deposit. He used it only for small purchases, like gas and school supplies, and made sure to pay the full balance each month. This helped him establish a record of on-time payments, which is the most important factor in a credit score.

To further build his credit, Alex took on a small bill in his own name. He set up a monthly phone plan that reported payments to credit bureaus. Since he had a part-time job at a local coffee shop, he set up automatic payments so he would never miss a due date.

Over time, Alex kept his credit utilization low, never spending more than 30% of his credit limit. By the time he was 19, he checked his credit score and saw that it was already above 700, a great score for someone his age. Because of this, when he went to lease his first apartment, he didn't need a co-signer like many of his friends did.

Now, at 20, Alex is working on his next financial goal: saving for a down payment on a car. Thanks to his responsible credit habits, he qualifies for lower interest rates, meaning he'll pay less over time compared to someone with a lower credit score.

By starting early, making smart choices, and staying disciplined, Alex set himself up for financial success. Instead of struggling with credit card debt like many young adults, he's using credit as a tool to create opportunities, not as a way to spend money he doesn't have.

You don't have to wait until adulthood to start building credit. Just like Alex, you can take small steps now, like becoming an authorized user, getting a secured credit card, paying bills on time, and keeping your credit usage low. These habits will put you ahead and give you financial freedom in the future.

Quick Quiz Box

True or False:

1. Using a credit card means you're spending your own money.
2. Paying only the minimum on your credit card helps you avoid debt.
3. A good credit score can help you get better interest rates and future opportunities.

(*Answers: F, F, T*)

Journal Reflection Box

Think of something you've borrowed, whether it was money, a book, or a game. How did it feel to be responsible for returning it? Now imagine borrowing money with interest, how would that change how you use it?

Action Challenge Chart

Task	Goal	Outcome
Learn what a credit score is	Understand how credit works	Build financial knowledge
Watch a video on credit cards	Learn how interest and payments work	Gain confidence with real-life tools
Talk to a parent about their first credit card	Hear a real experience	Learn lessons before making your own mistakes

Mini-FAQ: Credit & Debt Questions

Q1: What is credit, really?
A: Credit is borrowed money you agree to pay back later, often with interest. It can be useful if used wisely, or dangerous if misused.

Q2: Should teens worry about credit already?
A: Yes! What you do now (like becoming an authorized user or avoiding debt traps) can impact your financial future.

Q3: What's the biggest mistake teens make with credit?
A: Thinking it's free money. It's not. Always have a plan to pay it off, before you swipe.

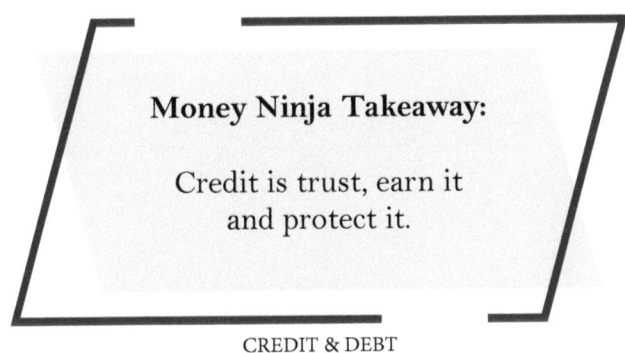

Money Ninja Takeaway:

Credit is trust, earn it and protect it.

PART II

SAVING

5

SAVINGS

The Power of Saving

Saving money is one of the most powerful financial habits you can develop. A Money Ninja knows that saving isn't about what you can't have, it's about what you can build. Every dollar you save gives you more choices and opportunities in the future. Whether it's buying your first car, traveling, starting a business, or simply having financial freedom, saving allows you to take control of your life and finances.

One of the easiest ways to manage money wisely is by following the 50/30/20 rule. This simple method helps you divide your income into three main categories: needs, wants, and savings.

- 50% goes to Needs – These are essential expenses such as food, transportation, rent, and bills.
- 30% goes to Wants – This is for fun things like eating out, video games, movies, hobbies, and entertainment.
- 20% goes to Savings & Investments – This money is set aside for your future, whether in a savings account, emergency fund, or investments.

For example, if you make $100 from a side hustle, you would allocate:
- $50 toward necessary expenses like groceries, gas, or school supplies.
- $30 for things you enjoy, such as going to the movies, buying new clothes, or eating out.
- $20 into savings or investments to help grow your financial future.

A Money Ninja always pays themselves first by saving before spending. Instead of using money on unnecessary purchases and saving whatever is left over, they make saving a priority. By following this mindset, they ensure that their financial goals come first, setting them up for a lifetime of financial security and freedom.

Savings Accounts

As a kid, you probably saved money in a piggy bank, dropping in spare change and watching your savings grow. That was a great start, it taught you the importance of putting money aside instead of spending it all at once. But now that you're older, it's time to graduate to a real savings account and start making your money work for you. Unlike a piggy bank, a savings account doesn't just store your money, it helps it grow.

One of the biggest advantages of a savings account is that it earns interest. This means the bank pays you money just for keeping your savings there. Over time, this interest compounds, allowing your balance to grow without you having to do anything. While interest rates may seem small at first, the longer your money stays in the account, the more it earns. Imagine putting away $500 in a savings account with a 2% interest rate, by doing nothing, you could end up with over $1,000 in just a few years if you keep adding to it and let it grow.

Another key benefit of a savings account is safety. Unlike keeping money in your room, where it could get lost, stolen, or accidentally spent, a bank protects your savings. Most banks are

FDIC-insured, which means even if the bank itself has financial trouble, your money (up to $250,000) is safe. This makes a savings account the smartest place to keep money you don't need for everyday spending.

Having a savings account also makes it easier to manage your money. With online banking, you can quickly transfer money between your checking and savings accounts, track your balance, and even set up automatic deposits so you're consistently saving without thinking about it. Some banks even allow you to create separate savings goals, for example, one fund for a new laptop, another for a car, and one for emergencies. This way, you stay organized and in control of your finances.

If you really want to make your money grow faster, consider opening a high-yield savings account. Unlike regular savings accounts, high-yield accounts offer higher interest rates, meaning your money earns even more over time. Many online banks, like Ally, Discover, and Marcus by Goldman Sachs, offer high-yield savings accounts with much better rates than traditional brick-and-mortar banks.

Talk to your parents or guardian about setting up your own savings account. Whether you open an account at a local bank or an online bank, taking this step will help you build strong financial habits early. The sooner you start saving in a real account, the sooner you'll be on your way to financial independence and freedom.

Needs Vs. Wants

Needs are the things you must have to live and function in your daily life. This includes food, transportation, housing, basic clothing, school supplies, and healthcare. Without these essentials, it would be difficult to survive or succeed. For example, buying a notebook and pencils for school is a need because they help you learn and complete your work. Paying for gas or a bus pass is also a need because it helps you get to work or school.

Wants, on the other hand, are things that bring comfort, entertainment, or status, but they are not essential for survival. These include designer clothes, the newest phone, eating fast food every day, or expensive gadgets. While these things may be enjoyable, they do not improve your long-term financial security. For example, upgrading to the latest iPhone every year may feel exciting, but if your current phone works just fine, that money could be better spent on savings or investments.

Before making a purchase, a Money Ninja asks themselves: Is this a need or a want? If it's a want, is it worth delaying financial goals for short-term satisfaction? Learning to make these distinctions helps prevent unnecessary spending and allows you to save for more important goals like a car, a business, or even future investments.

Spending Triggers: Why We Spend Without Thinking

Sometimes, we buy things without even realizing why. Our spending habits are often influenced by spending triggers, which can make us act on impulse instead of thinking logically about whether a purchase is necessary.

One of the biggest spending triggers is sales and discounts. Have you ever seen a "50% off" sale and felt like you had to buy something just because it was a great deal? Stores use this strategy to create a sense of urgency, making you feel like you're missing out if you don't buy now. However, if you weren't planning to buy that item in the first place, you didn't save money, you just spent money you didn't need to.

Peer pressure is another major spending trigger. If your friends are wearing the latest shoes, using the newest phone, or going out for expensive meals, you might feel pressured to keep up, even if it's not financially smart for you. A Money Ninja resists this pressure, knowing that true confidence comes from financial security, not from material possessions.

Another common trap is emotional spending, buying things because you're bored, sad, stressed, or even excited. Have you ever bought snacks, clothes, or gadgets just because you were feeling down? Retail therapy can feel good in the moment, but those purchases often lead to regret later. Instead of using shopping as a way to manage emotions, a Money Ninja finds other ways to cope, like going for a walk, talking to a friend, or practicing mindfulness.

Whenever you feel the urge to spend, pause for a moment and ask yourself: Do I really need this, or am I just reacting? This simple habit helps you make smarter money decisions instead of letting emotions or external pressure dictate how you spend.

A Money Ninja spends intentionally, they know that every dollar saved today is a step closer to financial freedom tomorrow. Instead of wasting money on things that don't truly matter, they focus on building wealth, making smart investments, and achieving long-term success.

How to Spot Good Deals vs. Scams

Not every deal is as good as it seems. Companies and advertisers use clever tactics to make you think you're getting a bargain when, in reality, you might be spending more than necessary, or even falling for a scam. A Money Ninja knows how to differentiate between a good deal and a marketing trick designed to make them spend impulsively.

A good deal is when you buy something you already planned to purchase but at a discounted price. For example, if you were already saving up for a laptop and find it on sale for 20% off, that's a smart purchase. A good deal also happens when you compare prices and find the best value for your money. Smart shoppers plan ahead, research prices, and only buy when they truly need something.

A scam, on the other hand, is a "too good to be true" offer that tricks people into spending money unnecessarily. Scams often come in the form of fake discounts, hidden fees, or pressure to buy something quickly before the deal disappears. If a company is forcing you to "act now" or making a deal sound urgent, that's a red flag. Scammers rely on creating panic and fear of missing out (FOMO) to get you to make poor financial decisions.

Businesses want you to spend money, and they use psychological tactics to encourage impulse buying. Even major retailers use these strategies to make you feel like you need something when you really don't.

One of the most effective tactics is FOMO (Fear of Missing Out). If you've ever seen a website flash a "Limited Time Only!"

sale or a countdown timer that makes you feel like you have to buy something right now, that's FOMO in action. Companies create fake urgency to pressure you into making a quick decision instead of thinking it through.

Another common trick is influencer hype. Social media influencers and celebrities are often paid to promote products, making them seem cooler or more valuable than they really are. If you see your favorite YouTuber or TikToker wearing a new brand of sneakers and suddenly feel like you need them too, ask yourself: Do I actually like these, or do I just want them because someone famous is wearing them?

Subscription traps are another sneaky way companies make money. They lure you in with offers like "First Month Free!" but hide the fact that canceling is extremely difficult. Many people sign up for free trials and forget to cancel, leading to months of unwanted charges. A Money Ninja always reads the fine print before signing up for any subscription and sets a reminder to cancel before the free trial ends.

Spending Wisely, Not Impulsively

Spending money isn't bad, but wasting money is. A Money Ninja doesn't just focus on finding the lowest price; they focus on getting the best value for their money. Just because something is on sale doesn't mean it's worth buying. Mindful spending helps you get what you truly need while avoiding unnecessary purchases.

One of the smartest habits is budgeting for fun. It's perfectly okay to enjoy your money, as long as you do it wisely. Setting aside a certain amount each month for entertainment, clothes, or gadgets lets you enjoy spending without guilt or financial stress.

Another powerful strategy I like to use is putting what I want in my cart and then waiting about a week to see if I still want it. Waiting at least 24 hours before making a big purchase is a good habit. If you see something you want, don't buy it right away. Instead, give yourself some time to think about whether you really need it. Often, you'll realize that the excitement fades, and you don't actually want it as much as you thought. This simple habit can save you hundreds, or even thousands, of dollars over time.

Finally, a Money Ninja knows that price doesn't always equal value. A cheap product that breaks easily is a waste of money, while a higher-quality item that lasts for years is often a better investment. For example, a $100 backpack that lasts five years is a better deal than a $20 backpack that falls apart after a few months. Learning to focus on quality over price helps you spend your money in ways that actually benefit you in the long run.

By thinking critically, avoiding impulse buying, and recognizing marketing tricks, you'll take control of your spending instead of letting companies manipulate your decisions. A Money Ninja is always aware, always intentional, and always in charge of their money.

Expert Advice

"Too many people spend money they haven't earned to buy things they don't want to impress people they don't like." — Will Rogers

Being smart with your money means understanding where it goes and not using banking tools recklessly.

Actionable Strategies

- Track your spending for a week – Write down every purchase to see where your money goes.
- Try a No-Spend Challenge – Go one week without buying anything unnecessary.
- Set a savings goal – Pick something specific (e.g., saving for a trip or a gadget) and start saving for it.

"A penny saved is a penny earned."
— BENJAMIN FRANKLIN

Personal Story: My First Savings Goal

When I was 14, I wanted a new bike. Instead of asking for money, I made a plan to save up for it. I skipped eating out, saved birthday money, and took on extra chores. It took me three months, but when I finally bought the bike, I felt amazing.

That bike meant more to me because I had worked and saved for it. That's when I realized: saving money isn't about what you don't buy, it's about what you can achieve.

Quick Quiz Box

True or False:

1. Needs and wants are the same thing.
2. A good deal always means you should buy something.
3. Saving money gives you more freedom.

(Answers: F, F, T)

Journal Reflection Box

Write about a time you saved for something. How did it feel when you finally bought it?

Action Challenge Chart

Task	Goal	Outcome
Track spending for a week	Identify spending habits	Become more mindful
Save $10 this week	Build a savings habit	Start small and grow
Avoid an impulse buy	Test delayed gratification	Keep more money in savings

Mini-FAQ: Savings Questions

Q1: What's the best way to start saving?
A: Set a small goal, like saving $5 a week, and build from there.

Q2: Do I need a savings account?
A: Yes! It's safer and earns interest, helping your money grow.

Q3: Is saving boring?
A: Not when you have a goal! Saving gives you more freedom and choices.

> **Money Ninja Takeaway:**
>
> Developing delayed gratification helps in every aspect of life: financial, personal, sports, career, and family.

6

GOAL-SETTING

Why Create a Plan

A Money Ninja knows that saving with a purpose is the secret to reaching big dreams. Whether it's buying your first car, saving for college, or planning a dream vacation, setting and reaching financial goals requires patience, discipline, and smart strategies.

Money without a plan often disappears quickly. But when you set a goal and work toward it, every dollar saved moves you closer to your dream.

Think about something you really want, maybe a gaming console, concert tickets, or your first car. Instead of just hoping you'll have enough money someday, set a clear savings goal and create a plan to achieve it.

Money Ninja's Secret to Wealth

One of the most powerful financial skills a Money Ninja can develop is delayed gratification, the ability to resist spending money impulsively today so you can reach a bigger, more meaningful goal in the future. While it may feel tempting to spend money the moment you get it, mastering delayed gratification separates financially successful people from those who always struggle with money.

Many people fall into the habit of instant gratification, where they make purchases based on wants rather than needs, spending money just because they have it. But a Money Ninja understands that small sacrifices now lead to greater rewards later. Instead of thinking, "I want this now!", they ask themselves, "Would I rather have this small thing today, or something much bigger and better later?"

A great example of delayed gratification is choosing to save money instead of spending it on temporary pleasures. Imagine you have $10 and you're tempted to buy fast food or a fancy coffee. That purchase will give you momentary satisfaction, but in a day or two, that money will be gone, and you'll have nothing to show for it.

Now imagine that instead of spending $10 every week on fast food, you save it instead. In just one month, you'd have $40, enough to buy something meaningful, like a new pair of high-quality shoes, a ticket to an event you've been wanting to attend, or even an investment in a business idea. Over a year, that small change in spending habits could save you over $500, enough to buy a new laptop, take a trip, or grow a savings account for something even bigger.

This is the secret that financially smart people understand: Short-term sacrifices create long-term success.

Delayed gratification isn't about depriving yourself, it's about making intentional choices with your money. When you say "no" to small, unnecessary purchases, you're actually saying "yes" to something much greater.

Think of it this way: Every time you resist spending money on something you don't really need, you're investing in your future self. That money could be used to start a business, buy something valuable, or create financial security.

For example, let's say you have a dream of owning your first car. If you save just $5 a day instead of spending it on impulse purchases, you'd have $1,825 saved up in just one year. That could be enough for a down payment on a used car or a huge step toward your goal.

This simple shift in thinking changes everything. Instead of feeling like you're missing out, you start to feel empowered, knowing that every dollar saved is bringing you closer to something important.

The ability to delay gratification isn't just about willpower, it's actually a skill that scientists say leads to higher levels of success, wealth, and happiness. A famous study known as The Marshmallow Experiment proved this.

In the study, researchers gave children a choice:

- They could eat one marshmallow immediately, OR
- If they waited just 15 minutes, they could have two marshmallows instead.

Years later, the researchers followed up with these kids. The ones who were able to wait for the second marshmallow were more successful in school, careers, relationships, and finances than those who took the instant reward.

The takeaway? People who can delay gratification are more likely to succeed in life because they know how to prioritize long-term goals over short-term pleasure.

As a Money Ninja, this means training yourself to think beyond today's wants and focus on tomorrow's success.

Just like any skill, delayed gratification gets easier with practice. Here are some ways to start strengthening your financial discipline:

1. Set Clear Financial Goals – It's easier to delay gratification when you have a specific goal in mind. Whether it's saving for a new phone, a car, or starting a business, remind yourself why you're saving.
2. Create a "Wish List" Instead of Buying Right Away – If you see something you want, write it down and wait 30 days. If you still want it after a month, then consider buying it. Often, you'll realize you don't actually need it.
3. Visualize Your Future Success – Picture yourself achieving your financial goals. When tempted to spend, ask yourself: "Will this bring me closer to my dream or take me further away?"

4. Make Saving Automatic – Set up an automatic transfer so part of your money goes straight into a savings account before you even see it. If you never have the chance to spend it, you won't miss it!
5. Reward Yourself Smartly – Delayed gratification doesn't mean never enjoying your money. It just means prioritizing. Give yourself small rewards for hitting savings goals to stay motivated.

A Money Ninja doesn't chase every short-term pleasure, they build toward long-term success. The ability to delay gratification separates those who struggle financially from those who achieve financial freedom. By making small sacrifices today, you set yourself up for a life with more choices, more opportunities, and more wealth.

The next time you're about to make an impulse purchase, pause and ask yourself:
"Is this helping me achieve my financial goals, or is it just a temporary pleasure?"

Your future self will thank you for the smart money decisions you make today. By practicing delayed gratification, you're already taking the first step toward financial success, but how do you turn that mindset into real, measurable progress? That's where P.P.O. (Process, Performance, Outcome) goals come in. Instead of just hoping to be better with money, this method gives you a clear roadmap to follow. It's my favorite way of setting financial goals because it's specific, actionable, and measurable, ensuring that you stay on track and actually see results.

How P.P.O. (Process, Performance, Outcome) Goals Can Help You Master Money

Setting financial goals is one of the most important steps in achieving financial success, but many people struggle with how to make their goals actionable and realistic. That's where the P.P.O. method, Process, Performance, and Outcome, comes in. This is my favorite way of creating goals. It's specific and the first two are measurable.

This system helps break down your financial goals into smaller, achievable steps, so you stay motivated and see real progress.

A Money Ninja doesn't just dream about being financially successful, they create a plan, track their progress, and adjust their strategy along the way. Let's dive into how Process, Performance, and Outcome goals can help you take control of your money.

Process Goals: The Daily Actions That Build Financial Success

Process goals are all about the actions and habits you develop, things you can control every single day. These are the small, consistent steps that, over time, lead to financial success. Instead of focusing on the big picture right away, process goals keep you focused on what you can do right now.

For example, if your ultimate goal is to save $1,000, a process goal might be:

- "I will put $10 into my savings account every week."
- "I will track my spending daily to see where my money is going."
- "I will make my own lunch instead of eating out three times a week."

These process goals focus on daily money habits, ensuring that your financial success isn't just a wish, it's a result of intentional action. The key is consistency. If you stick to these small daily habits, saving money will become automatic.

Performance Goals: Measuring Your Progress

Performance goals track how well you are executing your process goals. They help measure progress and ensure you're staying on the right track. While process goals focus on actions, performance goals focus on results within a specific timeframe.

For example, if your process goal is to save money every week, a performance goal could be:

- "I will save at least $40 per month for three months."

- "I will keep my monthly spending on non-essentials below $100."
- "I will reduce my eating-out expenses by 50% this month compared to last month."

Performance goals keep you accountable because they provide specific targets. If you don't reach a performance goal, you can analyze what went wrong, maybe your process goal needs adjusting, or you need to find new ways to cut expenses.

Outcome Goals: The Big Picture Financial Wins

Outcome goals are the end result you want to achieve, the major financial milestones that your process and performance goals help you reach. These goals focus on the long-term impact of your money habits.

Examples of outcome goals include:

- "I will save $1,000 in my emergency fund by the end of the year."
- "I will earn $500 a month from my side hustle within six months."
- "I will pay off $2,000 of my credit card debt in one year."

While outcome goals are exciting and provide a clear destination, they aren't completely in your control. You may face unexpected expenses or income fluctuations that slow your progress. That's why focusing on process and performance goals first is essential, these daily and short-term efforts ensure that you're consistently moving toward your long-term financial success.

How P.P.O. Goals Work Together to Build Wealth

Think of Process, Performance, and Outcome goals as a staircase leading to financial success.

1. Process goals are the steps you take every day, saving a little at a time, tracking your spending, cutting back on unnecessary expenses.
2. Performance goals track your progress, keeping you motivated and accountable. You can see whether you're saving enough each month or staying under budget.
3. Outcome goals are the final result, the financial success that comes from all the small, disciplined steps you've taken along the way.

A Money Ninja uses P.P.O. goals as a secret weapon for financial success. Instead of just hoping to "be better with money," they create a system that ensures they develop good habits, track their progress, and achieve major financial milestones.

So, what's your next P.P.O. financial goal? Start small, stay consistent, and watch how these three types of goals transform your money management skills.

Expert Advice

"Someone's sitting in the shade today because someone planted a tree a long time ago." — Warren Buffett

Saving may seem small now, but every dollar builds future security. Start planting seeds today.

Actionable Strategies

- Write down your savings goal – Be specific about what you're saving for.
- Find one way to cut spending – Put that money toward your goal instead.
- Track your savings progress – Watching your money grow keeps you motivated!

"A goal without a plan is just a wish."
– ANTOINE DE SAINT-EXUPÉRY

Personal Story: My First Big Savings Goal

When I was 15, I wanted my own laptop. My parents said they'd help, but I had to cover half of the cost. At first, it felt impossible. But I created a plan: I saved my birthday money, took on extra chores, and said no to buying snacks at school.

Six months later, I had enough money! When I finally bought the laptop, it wasn't just about the computer, it was about knowing I could achieve something if I worked for it. That lesson has stuck with me ever since.

Quick Quiz Box

True or False:

1. It's impossible to save for big goals as a teen.
2. Long-term goals take planning and patience.
3. Small savings don't make a difference.

(*Answers: F, T, F*)

Journal Reflection Box

What is one big goal you want to save for? What steps can you take to make it happen?

Action Challenge Chart

Task	Goal	Outcome
Set a savings goal	Give your money a purpose	Stay motivated to save
Save $5 a week	Build a habit	See your money grow over time
Avoid one unnecessary purchase	Practice delayed gratification	Feel empowered to reach bigger goals

Mini-FAQ: Goal-setting Questions

Q1: How do I stay motivated to save?
A: Keep your goal visible, make a vision board or savings tracker!

Q2: What if my goal feels too big?
A: Break it down into smaller steps so you can celebrate progress along the way.

Q3: Why does delayed gratification matter?
A: It helps you build patience and self-control, which are key to financial success.

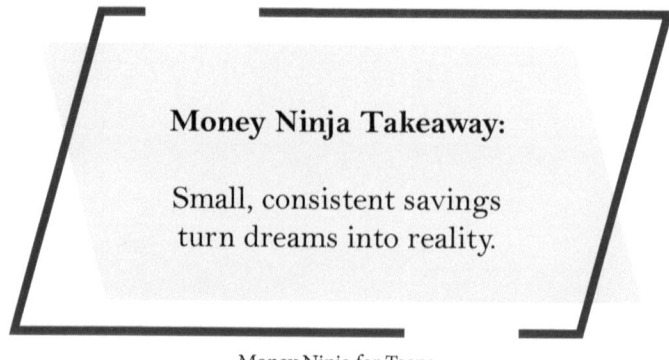

Money Ninja Takeaway:

Small, consistent savings turn dreams into reality.

GOAL-SETTING

PART III

INVEST

7

INVESTMENTS

Investing is Key

Saving money is important, but a Money Ninja knows that investing is the key to building long-term wealth. Investing allows your money to grow over time, giving your future self more financial security, freedom, and opportunities.

Investing means putting your money into something that can grow over time. Here are a some common types of investments:

1. Savings Accounts – A safe place to store money while earning a small amount of interest.
2. Stocks – Buying a small piece of a company. If the company does well, your stock increases in value.
3. Mutual Funds – A mix of different investments managed by professionals.
4. Starting a Business – Investing in yourself by creating a product or service that generates income.
5. Real Estate – Buying property to rent or sell later for a profit.

Savings Accounts

A savings account is the safest place to store your money while earning a small amount of interest. Unlike cash sitting in a piggy bank, money in a savings account grows slowly over time because banks pay you interest for keeping your money with them. While interest rates are low compared to other investments, savings accounts offer security, easy access to your money, and a great place to store emergency funds. Many banks also offer high-yield savings accounts, which pay slightly higher interest rates and help your money grow faster.

Stocks

When you buy a stock, you're buying a small piece of a company. If that company does well, the value of your stock increases, and you can sell it for a profit. However, if the company does poorly, the stock price may drop, and you could lose money. Stocks are a great long-term investment, and historically, they have provided high returns over time. Many well-known companies, like Apple, Tesla, and Nike, allow people to buy shares and become part-owners of the business. A Money Ninja invests in stocks wisely by researching companies and thinking long-term instead of trying to get rich overnight.

Mutual Funds

Mutual funds are a mix of different investments, like stocks and bonds, managed by professionals. Instead of buying a single stock, you invest in a fund that spreads your money across multiple companies. This reduces risk because even if one company in the fund doesn't do well, others might perform better and balance it out. Mutual funds are a great choice for beginners because they offer diversification (spreading out risk) and are managed by experts who make investment decisions for you.

Starting a Business

Investing isn't just about stocks and savings, it can also mean investing in yourself. Many successful entrepreneurs started by creating a small business that grew into something big. Whether it's selling handmade crafts, launching a YouTube channel, or offering tutoring services, starting a business allows you to generate income, build skills, and control your financial future. The key to a successful business is finding something you enjoy that solves a problem or adds value to others. A Money Ninja knows that building a business requires patience, creativity, and hard work, but the rewards can be life-changing.

Real Estate

Real estate is another powerful way to invest money and build wealth. This means buying property, such as a house or apartment, to rent out or sell later for a profit. Real estate values tend to increase over time, making it a great long-term investment. Some people start with house hacking, buying a small home, living in part of it, and renting out the rest to help cover the mortgage. Even though real estate requires more money upfront, it can provide passive income (money that comes in without daily work) and build financial stability over time.

Real estate is a great investment because it allows you to make money in three ways:

1. Appreciation – The property value increases over time, meaning you can sell it for more than you paid.
2. Collateral Access – You can borrow against the value of your property to fund other investments or business ventures.
3. Passive Income – Renting out your property brings in consistent monthly income without requiring daily effort.

A Money Ninja thinks ahead and looks at investing as a way to create long-term wealth, not just quick money. Whether through stocks, mutual funds, businesses, or real estate, making smart investment choices early on leads to financial freedom in the future.

The Magic of Compound Interest

One of the most powerful financial forces in the world is compound interest, the ability for money to grow exponentially over time. This is how investors, businesses, and financially successful people build wealth effortlessly. A Money Ninja understands that time is the key to unlocking the magic of compound interest, and the earlier you start, the greater your rewards will be.

So what exactly is compound interest, and why is it so powerful? Unlike simple interest, where you only earn money on your original investment, compound interest means that your interest earns interest too. This creates a snowball effect, where your money keeps growing at an increasing rate.

Let's say you invest $1,000 in an account that earns 10% annual interest.

- Year 1: You earn 10% of $1,000, which is $100, bringing your total to $1,100.
- Year 2: Instead of earning 10% on just your original $1,000, you now earn 10% on $1,100, which means you get $110 in interest. Your total is now $1,210.
- Year 3: You now earn 10% on $1,210, which adds another $121, bringing your total to $1,331.

At first, the growth might not seem like much, but the longer you let your money compound, the more powerful the effect becomes.

After 30 years, that original $1,000 investment would grow to over $17,000, without you adding a single extra dollar.

If you added just $100 per month to your investment, you'd have over $200,000 in 30 years!

This is the power of time and patience. The earlier you start, the more time compound interest has to work its magic.

Compound interest is like a snowball rolling down a hill, the sooner it starts rolling, the bigger it gets. If you wait until later in life to start investing, you miss out on the most powerful ingredient: TIME.

For example, let's compare two people:

- Emma starts investing $100 a month at age 18 and stops at 30. Even though she only invested for 12 years, she lets the money sit and grow. By the time she's 60, she has over $400,000, even though she only contributed $14,400!
- Liam waits until age 30 to start investing $100 a month and keeps investing until age 60. Even though he contributed for 30 years, he only ends up with around $300,000.

Even though Liam invested for much longer, Emma ended up with more money because she started earlier and let compound interest do the heavy lifting.

This is why a Money Ninja starts investing as early as possible, because time is the most valuable asset when it comes to wealth building.

To take full advantage of compound interest, you need three things:

1. Start Early – The sooner you start, the more time your money has to grow. Even investing small amounts now is better than waiting for the "perfect time."
2. Stay Consistent – Regularly adding money (even small amounts) supercharges compound interest. Whether it's $10, $50, or $100 a month, the key is to keep investing.
3. Let It Grow – The biggest mistake people make is withdrawing their money too soon. The longer you let it sit, the more it multiplies. A Money Ninja is patient, knowing that short-term gains don't compare to the power of long-term growth.

The biggest secret of the wealthy is they let their money work for them. Instead of trading time for money forever, they invest early and allow compound interest to build wealth over time.

A Money Ninja doesn't just save money, they invest it in places where it can grow, like high-yield savings accounts, stocks, index funds, and retirement accounts. The key is starting early and staying consistent, so your money has time to multiply.

So, what's stopping you? The best time to start was yesterday. The second-best time is today. Even if you start with just $10 a week, your future self will thank you for letting compound interest work its magic!

Accounts for Compound Interest Growth

Now that you understand the magic of compound interest, the next step is knowing where to put your money so it grows effectively. Not all accounts maximize compound interest, and choosing the right one depends on your goals, risk tolerance, and time horizon. A Money Ninja doesn't just save money, they invest it where it can grow. Here are the best types of accounts and investments that allow you to take advantage of compound interest:

1. High-Yield Savings Accounts: Safe & Steady Growth

A high-yield savings account (HYSA) is one of the safest places to store money while earning interest. Unlike a regular savings account, which may offer 0.01% interest (basically nothing), an HYSA can offer 4-5% interest per year, which makes a big difference over time.

- Best for: Emergency funds, short-term savings, and keeping cash secure.
- Pros: Low risk, FDIC-insured (up to $250,000), easy access.
- Cons: Growth is much slower compared to stocks or mutual funds.

Where to Open One: Online banks like Ally, Discover, SoFi, and Marcus by Goldman Sachs often offer higher interest rates than traditional banks.

2. Certificates of Deposit (CDs): Guaranteed Growth

A Certificate of Deposit (CD) is a low-risk investment where you deposit money for a fixed period (e.g., 6 months, 1 year, or 5 years) and earn a higher fixed interest rate. The longer you leave your money in, the higher the rate.

- Best for: Money you don't need right away but want to grow safely.
- Pros: Higher interest rates than savings accounts, guaranteed returns.
- Cons: You can't withdraw money early without penalties.

Where to Open One: Most banks and credit unions offer CDs, but online banks tend to have higher rates.

3. Mutual Funds & Index Funds: The Smart Way to Invest

If you want higher growth than savings accounts, mutual funds and index funds are excellent long-term investment options. Instead of picking individual stocks, these funds allow you to invest in a diversified portfolio of stocks and bonds, spreading out risk while maximizing growth.

- Best for: Long-term investing (5+ years), retirement, and building wealth.
- Pros: Hands-off investing, diversification, historically strong returns (7-10% annually).
- Cons: Some funds have fees, and the stock market can fluctuate in the short term.

Best Index Funds to Start With:

- Vanguard S&P 500 ETF (VOO) – Invests in the top 500 U.S. companies.
- Fidelity ZERO Total Market Index Fund (FZROX) – Low-cost fund with broad market exposure.
- Schwab Total Stock Market Index Fund (SWTSX) – Includes thousands of stocks for diversification.

4. Roth IRA & Traditional IRA: Tax-Free Compound Growth

A Roth IRA is one of the best ways to build wealth using compound interest while avoiding taxes. You contribute after-tax money, and your investments grow completely tax-free, meaning you don't have to pay taxes when you withdraw money in retirement.

A Traditional IRA works similarly, but you don't pay taxes upfront, instead, you pay when you withdraw in retirement.

- Best for: Retirement savings, long-term investing, and tax-free growth.
- Pros: Huge tax advantages, compound growth over decades, flexible investment choices.
- Cons: You can't withdraw before age 59½ without penalties (unless for special cases like a first-time home purchase).

How to Start: Open a Roth IRA or Traditional IRA with Fidelity, Vanguard, or Charles Schwab, and invest in index funds or ETFs.

5. Brokerage Accounts: Flexible Investing in Stocks & ETFs

A brokerage account allows you to invest in stocks, ETFs, bonds, and more without the restrictions of retirement accounts. While stocks offer higher growth potential, they are also more volatile, meaning the value can rise and fall.

- Best for: Growing wealth over time, investing in stocks, flexibility.
- Pros: No contribution limits, can buy/sell investments anytime.
- Cons: Gains are taxed, and stock values can drop short-term.

Where to Open One: Fidelity, Robinhood, TD Ameritrade, and Charles Schwab are great places to start.

6. 401(k) Plans: Free Money from Your Employer

If your job offers a 401(k) plan, this is a must-use for long-term investing. Many employers offer a 401(k) match, which means they give you free money for investing.

- Best for: Retirement savings, getting free money from employer contributions.
- Pros: Tax advantages, employer matching, automatic investing.
- Cons: Limited investment options, penalties for early withdrawal.
- Pro Tip: If your employer matches 401(k) contributions, always contribute at least enough to get the full match, it's free money!

How to Choose the Right Account for You

If you're saving for short-term goals (1-3 years):
➡ High-Yield Savings Account (HYSA) or CD

If you're investing for long-term growth (5+ years):
➡ Index Funds (S&P 500, Total Stock Market)

If you want tax-free retirement growth:
➡ Roth IRA or 401(k) with employer matching

If you want flexibility to invest freely:
➡ Brokerage account for stocks and ETFs

A Money Ninja knows that not all money should be stored in the same place. By diversifying between safe savings and high-growth investments, you can build financial security while letting compound interest do the work.

So, where will you start investing your money today?

Expert Advice

"Compound interest is the eighth wonder of the world." — Albert Einstein

Even small amounts of money can grow into big wealth if you start early and stay consistent.

Actionable Strategies

- Open an investment account – Ask a parent or guardian to help you open a beginner-friendly investment account.
- Start small – Even $5 or $10 a week can make a huge difference over time.
- Learn as you go – Follow investing podcasts, read books, or use free stock market simulation apps to practice before investing real money.

"Do not save what is left after spending, but spend what is left after saving."
– WARREN BUFFETT

Personal Story: My First Investment

When I was 16, I heard about investing but thought it was only for adults. Then I learned about index funds, a way to invest in the whole stock market instead of picking individual companies. I started with just $50, and within a year, my money had grown! It wasn't much at first, but seeing my money grow made me realize: investing is like planting a tree, the sooner you start, the bigger it grows.

Quick Quiz Box

True or False:

1. Investing is only for adults.
2. Compound interest helps money grow faster.
3. Real estate and businesses are advanced investments.

(Answers: F, T, T)

Journal Reflection Box

What's one thing you would invest in if you had $100? Why?

Action Challenge Chart

Task	Goal	Outcome
Research one investment type	Learn about stocks, funds, or real estate	Gain knowledge about growing money
Save $10 for investing	Start building an investment fund	Create a habit of investing
Learn about compound interest	Understand long-term investing	See the power of growing money over time

Mini-FAQ: Investments Questions

Q1: What's the best way for a teen to start investing?
A: Open a custodial investment account and start with index funds.

Q2: Is investing risky?
A: All investing has risks, but long-term investing in solid funds helps reduce risk.

Q3: How much money do I need to start investing?
A: You can start with as little as $5–$10 with apps designed for beginners.

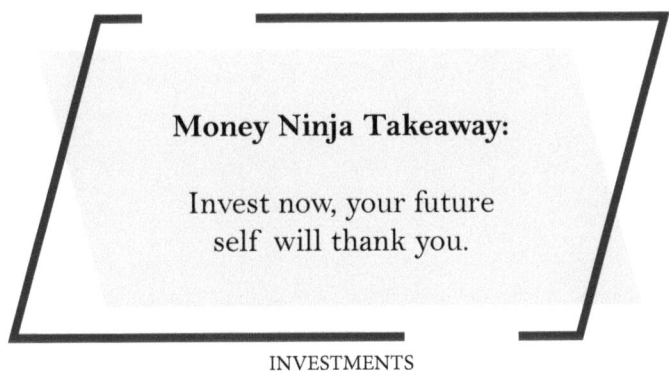

Money Ninja Takeaway:

Invest now, your future self will thank you.

8

ENTREPRENEURSHIP

4 F's of Entrepreneurship

A Money Ninja understands that entrepreneurship is a powerful way to create financial freedom by turning ideas into real businesses. Being an entrepreneur means finding a passion, solving a problem, and taking action to build something meaningful.

Successful entrepreneurs follow these four steps to turn their ideas into action:

1. Follow your passion – Choose something you love or enjoy doing.
2. Find a problem or need – Identify something people struggle with.
3. Fix a problem or fill the need – Offer a solution that helps others.
4. Form a business or organization – Turn your idea into a real business.

1. Follow Your Passion

The best businesses start with something you love. When you are passionate about your work, you are more likely to stay motivated, overcome challenges, and create something truly valuable. Passion fuels persistence, and in entrepreneurship, persistence is what separates those who succeed from those who give up.

Think about what excites you, maybe it's technology, art, sports, or helping others. Passionate entrepreneurs find a way to turn their interests into a business that makes an impact.

Example: Moziah Bridges loved fashion and bow ties, so at just 9 years old, he started Mo's Bows, a handmade bow tie business that grew into a national brand.

2. Find a Problem or Need

Every great business solves a problem or meets a need. The easiest way to come up with a business idea is to ask, *What do people struggle with? What is missing?* Successful entrepreneurs are problem-solvers who look for opportunities in everyday life.

A Money Ninja trains themselves to think like an entrepreneur by noticing pain points. Do your classmates always complain about losing their phone chargers? Do your neighbors struggle to find a pet sitter? These are business opportunities waiting to happen!

Example: Mikaila Ulmer saw that bees were disappearing at an alarming rate and wanted to help. She created Me & the Bees Lemonade, a business that sells honey-sweetened lemonade and donates profits to bee conservation.

3. Fix a Problem or Fill the Need

Once you've found a problem, the next step is creating a solution. Your business should make life easier, better, or more enjoyable for your customers.

Not every solution has to be complicated! Many businesses start with simple ideas, helping people save time, improving a product, or making something more affordable. The best businesses improve people's lives in some way, big or small.

Example: Ryan Kaji loved reviewing toys, so he started Ryan's World, a YouTube channel where he unboxes and tests toys. His fun, relatable content solved the problem of parents wondering which toys were worth buying. His brand expanded into merchandise, books, and more.

4. Form a Business or Organization

The final step in turning your idea into a real business is taking action. This means setting your prices, creating a simple business plan, and getting your first customers. Many successful entrepreneurs start small, selling to friends, family, and their local community before expanding to a wider audience.

Thanks to the internet, starting a business today is easier than ever. You can sell handmade products on Etsy, offer tutoring services through social media, design digital products, or launch a blog, podcast, or YouTube channel. The opportunities are endless, but the key is to stop waiting and start doing. A Money Ninja doesn't just dream about ideas, they bring them to life.

One inspiring example is Alina Morse, who was tired of dentists telling her that candy was bad for her teeth. Instead of accepting the problem, she created Zolli Candy, a line of sugar-free, tooth-friendly treats. She didn't just start a business; she built a brand that now sells in stores nationwide. Her success wasn't just about making money, it was about solving a problem, creating value for others, and turning a passion into a business.

But forming a business isn't just about selling, it's also about building a strong foundation. This means thinking about your brand, mission, vision, and legal protections.

A business is more than just a product or service, it's a brand. Your brand is what makes you unique, and it includes things like your logo, colors, messaging, and customer experience. When people see your business, they should immediately recognize what you stand for.

1. Logo & Design – A logo is the face of your brand. It should be simple, memorable, and represent your business identity.

You can create one using free tools like Canva or hire a designer on Fiverr or Upwork.
2. Trademarks & Legal Protection – If you create a unique brand name, logo, or slogan, you may want to trademark it to prevent others from copying it. In the U.S., this means registering with the United States Patent and Trademark Office (USPTO). Protecting your brand ensures that no one else can legally use your name or logo without permission.
3. Your Business Name – Choose a name that is easy to remember, represents your product or service, and isn't already taken. Before finalizing, check if the domain name (website URL) is available on GoDaddy or Namecheap and search the trademark database to avoid legal conflicts.

Defining Your Mission, Vision, and Values

A great business isn't just about selling, it's about having a clear purpose. Your mission, vision, and values define what your company stands for, why it exists, and what it hopes to achieve.

1. Mission Statement – This explains why your business exists and what it aims to do.
   » Example: "To create delicious, sugar-free candy that keeps kids' teeth healthy and makes parents happy." (Zolli Candy)
2. Vision Statement – This is about the future, what you want your business to become.
   » Example: "To become the leading global brand for healthy, sugar-free treats."
3. Core Values – These are the guiding principles of your business, such as:
   » Integrity – Always be honest with customers.
   » Quality – Create the best possible product.
   » Innovation – Always look for new and better ways to serve customers.

A Money Ninja builds businesses with purpose. Having a strong mission and clear values helps you stand out, build trust with customers, and stay focused on long-term success.

Simple Steps to Form Your Business

Validate Your Idea – Ask yourself: Does this solve a problem? Is there a demand for it? Get feedback from potential customers.

1. Make a Simple Business Plan – Outline what you'll sell, who your customers are, how much it will cost, and how you'll market it. It doesn't need to be complicated, just clear enough to guide you.
2. Set Prices and Costs – Research what similar products or services charge and set prices that allow you to make a profit.
3. Start Small & Get Your First Customers – Sell to friends, family, and your community first. Then, use social media or online platforms to reach more people.
4. Build Your Brand – Create a logo, choose colors, and define your mission. Make sure your business looks professional and stands out.
5. Consider Legal Protections – If you're serious about growing, think about trademarking your brand name and logo to prevent copycats.
6. Scale & Expand – Once you have a strong foundation, grow by reaching new customers, improving your product, and reinvesting profits.

Entrepreneurship isn't just about making money, it's about creating value for others while doing something you love. The best businesses start by solving a problem, filling a gap in the market, or improving something people already use.

A Money Ninja looks at the world differently. Instead of complaining about a problem, they ask, "How can I fix this? How can I create something better?"

So, what problem will you solve? What business idea will you bring to life? The best time to start is NOW, because the sooner you take action, the sooner you can build something amazing.
Some of the best businesses start from hobbies or passions. Here are some examples:

- Love to bake? Sell homemade cookies or cupcakes.
- Great at drawing? Offer custom artwork or design services.
- Tech-savvy? Help people with website creation or social media.
- Enjoy writing? Start a blog, write eBooks, or offer tutoring.
- Like pets? Start a pet-sitting or dog-walking business.

A Money Ninja knows that doing what you love + helping others = a successful business.

Simple Marketing Strategies for Teens

Marketing is how you get people to notice and buy what you offer. Even if you have the best product or service, if no one knows about it, you won't make sales. The good news is that marketing doesn't have to be complicated or expensive. Here are some simple and effective ways to promote your business:

Social media is one of the most powerful marketing tools for teens. Platforms like Instagram, TikTok, and Facebook allow you to showcase your products or services for free. Posting pictures, short videos, or tips related to your business can help attract customers. Engage with your audience by responding to comments, using trending hashtags, and creating fun content that people want to share. A Money Ninja knows that consistent posting builds brand awareness over time.

1. Word of Mouth One of the easiest ways to get customers is by telling people you already know. Start by talking about your business with family, friends, classmates, and teachers. If they like what you offer, they will tell others. Word of mouth is powerful because people trust recommendations from

those they know. The more people talk about your business, the more likely new customers will find you.
2. Flyers & Posters Even in the digital age, physical marketing still works! Create eye-catching flyers or posters and place them where potential customers will see them, schools, local stores, community centers, or coffee shops. Keep the design simple, include your business name, a short description of what you offer, and contact information. A Money Ninja makes it easy for people to take action.
3. Referral Discounts Encouraging happy customers to refer their friends is a great way to grow your business. Offer a discount, freebie, or small reward to customers who bring in new business. For example, if you sell baked goods, you could offer "Buy 3, Get 1 Free" to anyone who refers a friend. People love getting rewards, and it encourages them to spread the word faster.
4. Join Local Events School fairs, farmers' markets, and community events are perfect opportunities to showcase your business. Setting up a small booth or table lets people see, test, and buy your product in person. Many successful businesses started by selling at local events before expanding. A Money Ninja knows that getting in front of people builds trust and creates loyal customers.

The key to marketing is being consistent and passionate about your mission, keep talking about your business, and people will start paying attention!

Expert Advice

"Opportunities don't happen. You create them." — Chris Grosser

Don't wait for someone to hand you a job. Be creative, take initiative, and build your own path to earning.

Actionable Strategies

4 F's of Entrepreneurship

1. **Follow** your passion – Choose something you love or enjoy doing.
2. **Find** a problem or need – Identify something people struggle with.
3. **Fix** a problem or fill the need – Offer a solution that helps others.
4. **Form** a business or organization – Turn your idea into a real business.

"**The** best way to predict the future is to create it."
— ABRAHAM LINCOLN

Personal Story: My Son's First Business

When my son was 14, he started a small business washing cars. He printed flyers, told neighbors, and set a price. At first, he only had a few customers, but after a couple of weeks, word spread, and he was making real money. He learned that starting is the hardest part, but once you take action, things start happening. That small business taught him the power of effort, consistency, and customer service.

Quick Quiz Box

True or False:

1. You need a lot of money to start a business.
2. The best businesses solve problems.
3. Passion alone is enough to build a business.

(Answers: F, T, F)

Journal Reflection Box

If you could start any business, what would it be and why?

Action Challenge Chart

Task	Goal	Outcome
Come up with a business idea	Identify your passion	Find an opportunity to create value
Find your first customer	Start small	Gain confidence as an entrepreneur
Promote your idea	Spread the word	Attract new customers

Mini-FAQ: Entrepreneurship Questions

Q1: What if I don't know what business to start?
A: Start by thinking about what you enjoy doing and how it can help others.

Q2: How much money do I need to start a business?
A: Many businesses start with little to no money, just creativity and effort!

Q3: What if I fail?
A: Every entrepreneur faces challenges. Learn from mistakes and keep going!

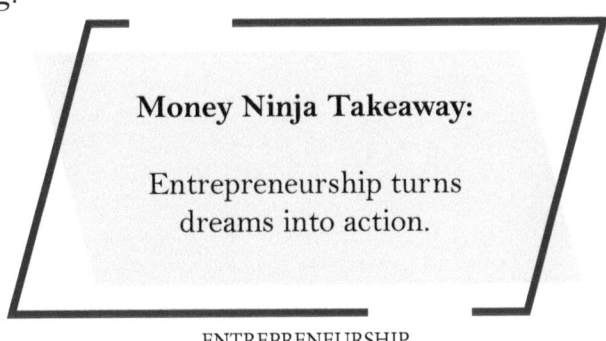

Money Ninja Takeaway:

Entrepreneurship turns dreams into action.

PART IV

DONATE

9

GENEROSITY

A Money Ninja understands that true wealth isn't just about what you have, it's about how you use it to help others. Generosity isn't just for millionaires and billionaires; it's for everyone. Whether you have a lot or a little, the way you share your resources, whether it's money, time, or skills, can make a real impact in the lives of others.

Many people think that giving is only for those who are already financially successful, but the truth is, generosity has nothing to do with how much money you have. It's a mindset, a way of using what you have to make life better for someone else. Even small acts of kindness can create ripple effects that spread through families, communities, and even the world.

Studies have shown that giving increases happiness, builds stronger relationships, and creates a deep sense of fulfillment. When you give, you don't just change someone else's life, you change your own. A Money Ninja knows that wealth is not measured by what you get, but by what you give.

Why Generosity Matters

Money is a powerful tool, but the true value is in how you use it. A Money Ninja understands that giving is an investment, not just in others, but in their own personal growth and happiness. Here's why generosity is so important:

1. Giving Strengthens Communities

When people support each other, communities thrive. Whether it's donating to a local food bank, providing school supplies for kids, or helping an elderly neighbor with their groceries, generosity creates stronger connections. A Money Ninja knows that a wealthy community benefits everyone, and they look for ways to give back to build a better future for all.

2. Generosity Creates More Opportunities

Helping others doesn't just benefit them, it also creates new opportunities for you. When you give your time, money, or skills, you build relationships that can lead to job opportunities, mentorship, or unexpected rewards. Many successful entrepreneurs and professionals got life-changing opportunities because they were known for being generous and helping others.

3. Giving Improves Mental and Emotional Well-being

Science proves that giving makes people happier. Studies show that acts of generosity trigger the release of endorphins, the same chemicals that make you feel happy after exercising. People who give regularly tend to have lower stress levels, greater life satisfaction, and even live longer!

A Money Ninja understands that true happiness doesn't come from material things, it comes from making a difference in the lives of others.

Ways to Give Back Wisely

Being generous doesn't mean giving away all your money without thinking. Smart giving means making the biggest impact with what you have. A Money Ninja chooses giving opportunities that truly matter and align with their values. Here's how:

1. Donate to Charities That Matter to You

If you have money to give, donate to organizations that support causes you believe in. Some people love helping children's education, others care about animal shelters, environmental conservation, or medical research. The key is to give where your heart is.

Before donating, a Money Ninja researches charities to make sure they are legitimate and that their money is actually going to the cause. Websites like Charity Navigator and GuideStar can help you find highly rated charities that use donations wisely.

2. Support Local Communities

Helping your own community is one of the most impactful ways to give. Here are a few ways to help locally:

- Donate school supplies, clothes, or hygiene kits to shelters.
- Volunteer at a food bank or serve meals to those in need.
- Support small businesses by shopping locally.

A Money Ninja looks for ways to make an impact close to home because a strong community helps everyone succeed.

3. Perform Acts of Kindness

Generosity isn't just about money, small acts of kindness can make someone's day better. Simple things like:

- Paying for someone's coffee in line behind you.
- Helping a neighbor with yard work.
- Tutoring a younger student who needs help in school.

Acts of kindness may seem small, but they create ripple effects of generosity. A Money Ninja knows that even the smallest action can inspire others to give too. Kindness is contagious and it starts with you.

Balancing Generosity with Smart Money Management

Giving is important, but a Money Ninja knows that generosity should never put them in financial hardship. The key is to give wisely while still taking care of your own financial goals.

1. Set a Giving Budget

One of the best ways to give responsibly is to decide ahead of time how much of your money will go toward helping others.
A simple rule is the 50/30/20 Rule:

- 50% for needs (rent, food, transportation).
- 30% for wants (entertainment, hobbies).
- 20% for savings, investing, and giving.

Some Money Ninjas set aside 5-10% of their income for giving. This way, they know exactly how much they can donate without affecting their own financial security.

2. Give Your Time If You Can't Give Money

Not everyone has extra money to donate, but giving your time is just as valuable! Many charities, shelters, and schools need volunteers to help. Even something as simple as teaching a free workshop, cleaning up a park, or mentoring someone younger can make a big difference.
A Money Ninja knows that time is one of the most valuable gifts, and sometimes, it's even more impactful than money.

3. Find Creative Ways to Give

If you run a business or side hustle, you can build giving into your work. Some businesses donate part of their sales to charity, while others organize fundraisers or sponsor community events.

For example:

- A baker could donate a portion of cupcake sales to a local shelter.
- A graphic designer could offer free logo design for nonprofit organizations.
- A personal trainer could host a charity fitness event where all proceeds go to a cause.

A Money Ninja thinks creatively about how to incorporate generosity into their life and work.

A Money Ninja understands that wealth isn't just about what you have, it's about how you use it to make the world better.

Generosity doesn't require being rich. It starts with a giving mindset, choosing to use what you have to help others, whether it's money, time, or talent. The greatest rewards in life don't come from accumulating more, they come from sharing and making a difference.

The next time you have an opportunity to give, whether it's helping a friend, donating to a cause, or simply showing kindness, take it. Because in the end, a Money Ninja measures wealth not by how much they keep, but by how much they give.

Expert Advice

"Beware of little expenses; a small leak will sink a great ship."
— Benjamin Franklin

Small, mindless spending can destroy even the best budget. Keep your habits tight like a ninja's focus.

Actionable Strategies

- Pick a cause you care about – Research organizations or local efforts you can support.
- Set aside a percentage of your income for giving – Even 5% can make a difference over time.

- Look for non-monetary ways to give – Volunteering, mentoring, and spreading awareness are valuable contributions.

"**No** one has ever become poor by giving."
– ANNE FRANK

Personal Story: My First Experience with Giving

When I was younger, I had a small business selling homemade bracelets. One day, I decided to donate a portion of my earnings to a local animal shelter. I didn't think it was much, but the shelter was incredibly grateful. They told me that my donation helped feed a dozen stray animals for a week. That was the moment I realized that even a small act of generosity can make a big impact.

Quick Quiz Box

True or False:

1. You have to be rich to give back.
2. Giving helps build stronger communities.
3. Donating time is just as valuable as donating money.

(Answers: F, T, T)

Journal Reflection Box

What is one way you can give back to your community this month?

Action Challenge Chart

Task	Goal	Outcome
Choose a charity to support	Find a cause you believe in	Make a meaningful impact
Volunteer for one hour	Give time instead of money	Strengthen community ties
Set a giving goal	Donate a small portion of income	Build generosity as a habit

Mini-FAQ: Generosity Questions

Q1: Do I have to give money to be generous?
A: No! Time, kindness, and skills are just as valuable.

Q2: How do I choose where to donate?
A: Find a cause that matters to you and research reputable organizations.

Q3: What if I don't have much to give?
A: Small acts of kindness, like volunteering or helping a neighbor, are powerful ways to give back.

Money Ninja Takeaway:

True wealth includes lifting others along the way.

PART V

CONCLUSION TO MONEY NINJA

10

PROTECT YOUR MONEY LIKE A NINJA

A Money Ninja doesn't just focus on earning and growing wealth, they also protect it fiercely, just like a ninja guards their secrets. Keeping your money safe is just as important as making it. If you don't take precautions, all your hard work, savings, and financial goals could be at risk.

In today's world, money can be stolen in more ways than ever. Whether it's online fraud, phone scams, identity theft, or careless financial habits, criminals and hackers are always looking for ways to take what's yours. But a Money Ninja is always aware, cautious, and prepared to fight off these threats.

One of the first steps to keeping your money safe is understanding the right way to handle your bank accounts and cards. Banks and credit card companies work hard to prevent fraud, but it's also up to you to be responsible and alert.

Here's how a Money Ninja keeps their banking information secure:

1. Keep Your Debit & Credit Card Information Private – Never share your card numbers, PINs, or security code with anyone. Even friends or family should never have access to your PIN.

2. Use Strong Passwords for Banking Apps – Avoid using easy-to-guess passwords like "123456" or "password". Instead, use a mix of letters, numbers, and symbols, and never reuse passwords across multiple sites.
3. Enable Alerts on Your Bank Account – Many banks allow you to set up text or email alerts when there's a withdrawal or suspicious activity on your account. If something looks off, you can act immediately.
4. Check Your Bank Statements Regularly – A Money Ninja always monitors their financial health. Log into your bank account at least once a week to check for unauthorized transactions. The sooner you catch fraud, the easier it is to fix!

Fraud Prevention: Recognizing Scams Before They Happen

Scammers are everywhere, and they are always coming up with new ways to trick people into giving away their money or personal information. A Money Ninja is always skeptical of anything that seems too good to be true or feels urgent and suspicious.

Here's how to avoid becoming a victim of fraud:

1. Be Cautious of Calls, Texts, or Emails Asking for Personal Information – If someone calls and claims to be from your bank, never give out your PIN, passwords, or Social Security number. Banks and government agencies will NEVER ask for personal details over the phone.
2. Don't Click on Suspicious Links – Scammers often send fake emails or texts that look real but are designed to steal your information. If you receive an email saying your bank account has been locked, don't click the link, go directly to your bank's website and log in.
3. Watch Out for Mail & Phone Fraud – Some scammers pretend to be from your bank or credit card company and will ask you to confirm your account details. If you're unsure, hang up and call the official number on your bank's website.

4. Never Wire Money or Pay with Gift Cards for Unverified Requests – Scammers often demand money in unusual ways, such as wire transfers or prepaid gift cards. No legitimate business or government agency will ever ask you to pay this way.

Understanding Financial Safety Online

Since so much of our financial life happens online, keeping your accounts secure is more important than ever. Hackers are constantly trying to break into accounts, steal credit card numbers, or sell personal data on the dark web.

A Money Ninja takes online security seriously and follows these essential steps:

1. Use Two-Factor Authentication (2FA) – This adds an extra layer of security to your accounts. Even if someone steals your password, they won't be able to log in without the second security step.
2. Monitor Your Bank Statements & Credit Reports – Regularly check your bank and credit card accounts for any strange transactions. If you see something you don't recognize, report it immediately.
3. Be Careful Where You Shop Online – Only enter your card information on websites that are secure (look for "https://" in the web address). If a website looks sketchy or unprofessional, don't take the risk.
4. Avoid Using Public Wi-Fi for Banking – Hackers can intercept public Wi-Fi connections and steal your banking details. A Money Ninja never logs into banking apps or enters sensitive information while on public networks.

Building an Emergency Fund: Your Financial Safety Net

A Money Ninja always has a backup plan! An emergency fund is one of the best ways to protect yourself from unexpected expenses. Whether it's a medical bill, car repair, or even job loss, having money saved gives you peace of mind and prevents you from going into debt when something unexpected happens.

How to Build an Emergency Fund (Teen-Friendly Steps):

1. Start Small: If saving $1,000 sounds overwhelming, start with a goal of $100, then work your way up to $500 or more.
2. Save a Little at a Time: Even putting away $5 or $10 a week adds up quickly. Small amounts may not seem like much now, but over time, they create financial security.
3. Keep It Separate: Open a separate savings account just for emergencies. That way, you're not tempted to spend it on other things.
4. Automate Your Savings: Many banks allow you to automatically transfer money from your checking account to savings. A Money Ninja makes saving effortless!

Having an emergency fund means you won't have to rely on credit cards or loans when life throws you a financial curveball.

The Money Ninja's Ultimate Protection Plan

A Money Ninja is always aware, always cautious, and always ready to defend their wealth from scammers, hackers, and bad financial decisions.

By following these steps, you'll be able to protect your money and future:

1. Be Smart with Your Bank Accounts – Keep your card details private, use strong passwords, and enable alerts on your account.
2. Learn to Spot Scams – Never give out personal information over the phone or email, and be wary of offers that seem too good to be true.
3. Secure Your Online Accounts – Use two-factor authentication, shop only on secure websites, and never use public Wi-Fi for banking.

4. Build an Emergency Fund – Always have savings set aside so you don't have to rely on credit cards or loans in tough situations.
5. Stay Aware & Educated – The more you learn about money safety and fraud prevention, the harder it will be for anyone to take advantage of you.

A Money Ninja doesn't just earn and grow money, they protect it like a fortress. By taking the right steps now, you'll be able to keep your wealth safe for the future!

Expert Advice

"An ounce of prevention is worth a pound of cure." — Benjamin Franklin

Protecting your money is just as important as earning it. Take simple steps now to avoid big problems later.

Actionable Strategies

- Set up strong passwords – Use a mix of letters, numbers, and symbols to secure accounts.
- Start an emergency fund – Set a small goal, like saving $50, and build from there.
- Be cautious with online purchases – Only buy from websites that you know and trust.

> "Do not save what is left after spending, but spend what is left after saving."
> – WARREN BUFFETT

Personal Story: The Time I Almost Fell for a Scam

A few years ago, I got a text that looked like it was from my bank. It said there was a "problem" with my account and asked me to click a link to fix it. Luckily, I stopped to think before clicking. Instead, I logged into my bank app directly and saw that my account was fine. It turned out to be a scam trying to steal my information! That experience taught me that staying cautious and thinking before acting is the best way to protect your money.

Quick Quiz Box

True or False:

1. You should always share your PIN with family members.
2. Scammers never try to steal personal information through emails or texts.
3. An emergency fund helps you prepare for unexpected expenses.

(Answers: F, F, T)

Journal Reflection Box

What's one way you can improve your financial security today?

Action Challenge Chart

Task	Goal	Outcome
Change weak passwords	Secure online accounts	Reduce risk of hacking
Start an emergency fund	Build financial safety	Be prepared for the unexpected
Learn about fraud	Avoid scams	Keep money safe

Mini-FAQ: Generosity Questions

Q1: Why do I need to protect my money if I don't even have that much yet?
A: Because every dollar counts. Whether you have $10 or $1,000, learning how to protect what you have now builds strong habits that will pay off big-time later. Identity theft, scams, and even simple spending mistakes can affect anyone, even teens. The sooner you learn to guard your money, the more confident and in control you'll be as your wealth grows.

Q2: Why should I care about passwords and digital safety?
A: Because your money lives online now, just like you. If someone hacks your accounts, they could steal your money, rack up charges in your name, or mess with your financial future. Creating strong passwords, not sharing your PIN, and being smart about what you click on protects your digital wallet like a true Money Ninja.

> **Money Ninja Takeaway:**
>
> Protect your wealth like a ninja protects their secrets.

11

MONEY PITFALLS NINJAS CAN AVOID

Even the smartest Money Ninjas make mistakes, but the key is to learn from them. No one is born a financial expert. The path to financial success is filled with trial and error, and every mistake is an opportunity to become wiser, stronger, and more financially secure. Understanding common money pitfalls will help you make better financial choices, avoid unnecessary stress, and build a strong foundation for the future.

Many teens (and even adults) fall into money traps without realizing it. The good news? Once you recognize these common financial missteps, you can avoid them and stay ahead of the game. Let's break down some of the biggest money mistakes and how a Money Ninja can overcome them.

1. Impulse Spending: The Silent Money Killer

One of the most common financial traps is impulse spending, buying things on a whim instead of sticking to a plan. Marketers love to tempt you with limited-time sales, flashy ads, and the feeling of "needing" something right now. But most impulse purchases don't bring lasting happiness, and they drain your wallet fast.

Mistake: Buying something the moment you see it, without thinking about whether you actually need it.

Money Ninja Strategy: Wait 24 hours before making non-essential purchases. If you still want it after a day, then it might be worth buying. This gives you time to think logically instead of emotionally.

Pro Tip: Create a "wishlist" instead of buying things instantly. After a month, look at the list, most of the time, you won't even want those things anymore!

2. Not Saving Early: The "I'll Do It Later" Trap

Many people think, "I'll start saving when I have more money." But the truth is, saving is a habit, not a number. The earlier you start, even with just a little, the easier it will be to build wealth over time.

Mistake: Thinking you have plenty of time to save later, so you don't start now.

Money Ninja Strategy: Start small, save $5 or $10 a week. Over time, it adds up! The sooner you begin, the more compound interest works in your favor.

Pro Tip: Set up automatic transfers so a small amount goes into savings every time you get money. You won't even miss it, but your future self will thank you!

3. Ignoring Budgets: Losing Track of Your Money

If you don't know where your money is going, you'll always feel broke, even if you're earning money. Without a budget, you'll spend money randomly, run out faster than expected, and struggle to afford the things that truly matter.

Mistake: Spending without tracking your money, which leads to financial stress.

Money Ninja Strategy: Use a simple budgeting method like the 50/30/20 rule:

- 50% for needs (rent, food, transportation)

- 30% for wants (fun, hobbies, entertainment)
- 20% for savings and investments

Pro Tip: Use budgeting apps like Mint, YNAB, or Goodbudget to help track where your money goes.

4. Relying on Credit Without a Plan

Credit cards can be useful tools, but they can also lead to debt traps if not used responsibly. Many people think of credit as "free money" and don't realize that borrowing comes with high-interest rates.

Mistake: Borrowing money without knowing how to pay it back.

Money Ninja Strategy: Only use credit cards for what you can afford to pay off in full each month. If you can't pay off the balance, don't swipe the card!

Pro Tip: If you use a credit card, set up automatic payments so you never miss a due date and avoid expensive late fees.

Learning from Financial Setbacks

Nobody's perfect, and financial mistakes happen to everyone. Even successful business owners and millionaires have made money mistakes, but what separates them is that they learn from them and improve.

A Money Ninja doesn't waste time feeling guilty about financial missteps. Instead, they reflect, adjust, and move forward smarter.

- Reflect on What Happened – Did you overspend? Forget to save? Not research a purchase? Understanding why the mistake happened helps you prevent it in the future.
- Create a Plan to Fix It – If you overspent, find ways to cut back until you're back on track. If you didn't save enough, set a small weekly savings goal to start building your habit.

- Stay Positive – Every mistake is a chance to grow. Even the most successful people made financial errors before they mastered money. The key is to keep improving!

Pro Tip: Keep a money journal where you write down any mistakes you make and what you learned from them. This will help you see patterns and avoid repeating the same errors.

Developing a Healthy Attitude Toward Money Mistakes

The way you think about mistakes shapes how you handle them. A Money Ninja doesn't see failure as defeat, they see it as a stepping stone to financial mastery.

1. Mistakes Are Lessons, Not Failures

Instead of being upset about a mistake, ask yourself:

- What did I learn from this?
- How can I make a better choice next time?

2. Money is a Skill, Practice Makes Perfect

Just like learning a sport, an instrument, or a martial art, the more you practice managing money, the better you'll get. No one expects to be a perfect basketball player the first time they shoot a hoop, why expect perfection with money?

3. Your Future Self Will Thank You

Every mistake you correct now makes you smarter and stronger financially in the future. The best thing you can do is learn fast and apply what you've learned to make smarter choices going forward.

Pro Tip: Set a "money mindset reminder", a sticky note or phone reminder that says something like:

Every money mistake is a chance to learn and grow!

No one is perfect with money, but the difference between struggling financially and building wealth is how you respond to mistakes. A Money Ninja knows that learning from failures is the key to success.

- Recognize common money mistakes (impulse spending, not saving, ignoring budgets, relying on credit).
- Take responsibility, adjust, and create a plan to fix past mistakes.
- Develop a healthy attitude toward failure, mistakes are just stepping stones to financial mastery!

The more you learn from each experience, the stronger your financial future will be. So, the next time you make a money mistake, don't get discouraged, get smarter!

Expert Advice

"The only real mistake is the one from which we learn nothing."
— Henry Ford

Everyone makes money mistakes. What matters is learning from them and becoming wiser with each one.

Actionable Strategies

- Track one financial mistake this month – Write down what went wrong and how you can avoid it next time.
- Set a mini financial goal – Example: Save $20, avoid impulse spending for a week, or track your expenses.
- Talk about money – Ask a parent, teacher, or mentor about a financial mistake they learned from and what they did differently.

"**Failure** is simply the opportunity to begin again, this time more intelligently."
– HENRY FORD

Personal Story: The Time I Wasted Money

When I first started earning money, I spent it all on fast food and random things I didn't need. One month, I realized I had nothing left to show for it. That's when I learned the power of tracking my spending. Now, every time I'm about to buy something, I ask myself: *Will this still be important a month from now?* If the answer is no, I skip it. That small mindset shift has saved me hundreds of dollars.

Quick Quiz Box

True or False:
1. Mistakes with money mean you'll never be good at managing it.
2. Overspending once in a while isn't a big deal as long as you learn from it.
3. Credit cards should be used without a plan.

(*Answers: F, T, F*)

Journal Reflection Box

What is one financial mistake you've made? What did you learn from it?

Action Challenge Chart

Task	Goal	Outcome
Reflect on a past money mistake	Learn from experience	Gain wisdom and avoid repeating it
Track impulse purchases for 7 days	Spot emotional or unnecessary spending	Build awareness and control
Create a "Don't Buy" list	Avoid common spending traps	Reduce regrets and save more money
Talk to a trusted adult about a financial mistake they made	Gain perspective	Learn valuable lessons from others

Mini-FAQ

Q1: What if I already made a money mistake? Is it too late?
A: Not at all! Mistakes are how you learn. Even adults mess up with money. What matters is that you figure out what went wrong, then make a better decision next time.

Q2: How do I know if I'm falling into a bad money habit?
A: If you're spending without thinking, ignoring your budget, or feeling regret after purchases, that's your signal. Hit pause, check your mindset, and course-correct like a true Ninja.

Q3: What's the worst money mistake teens make?
A: Thinking it's "not a big deal." Habits start now. Even small choices, like saving instead of spending, can shape your future in a big way.

Money Ninja Takeaway:

Mistakes aren't the end, they're stepping stones to financial mastery.

12

YOUR MONEY FUTURE

Becoming a Money Ninja is a journey, one that requires discipline, knowledge, and action. Throughout this book, you've learned the essential skills of a Money Ninja: how to earn, save, invest, and protect your wealth while making a difference in the world. Now, it's time to bring everything together and create a game plan for your financial future.

A Money Ninja doesn't leave their future to chance. They set goals, make smart financial decisions, and take consistent action to build a life of financial freedom. Let's review the key lessons from this journey so you can continue sharpening your financial skills and mastering your money.

Part I: Introduction to Money Ninja

Chapter 1: What is a Money Ninja?

A Money Ninja is someone who understands that money is a tool, not just for spending, but for creating opportunities, security, and freedom. A Money Ninja isn't just about getting rich; they're about being smart with money so they can live life on their own terms.

Chapter 2: Money Mindset

Your mindset affects your financial success. A Money Ninja develops a strong money mindset by understanding the difference between assets and liabilities, practicing delayed gratification, and setting financial goals that align with their dreams.

Chapter 3: Earnings

Earning money is the foundation of financial independence. A Money Ninja builds multiple income streams, chooses work that aligns with their values, and isn't afraid to take action, whether through jobs, side hustles, or business opportunities.

Chapter 4: Credit & Debt

Credit can be a powerful tool or a dangerous trap. A Money Ninja uses credit wisely, avoids unnecessary debt, and understands the magic (and danger) of compound interest. They always have a plan for repayment and never borrow more than they can afford to pay back.

Part II: SAVE

Chapter 5: Savings

A Money Ninja knows that saving money isn't about restriction, it's about freedom. The 50/30/20 rule helps balance needs, wants, and savings. A Money Ninja also builds an emergency fund so they're prepared for unexpected expenses.

Chapter 6: Goal-setting

Big financial goals require planning and determination. Whether it's saving for college, a car, or a business, a Money Ninja sets clear, realistic, and measurable goals to make it happen.

Part III: INVEST

Chapter 7: Investments

The secret to building wealth is investing. A Money Ninja understands compound interest, knows the importance of starting early, and invests in stocks, index funds, and retirement accounts to grow their money over time.

Chapter 8: Entrepreneurship

Entrepreneurship allows Money Ninjas to create their own opportunities. Whether it's starting a business, building a brand, or investing in an idea, they take risks wisely and learn from every experience. A Money Ninja knows that financial freedom comes from creating value for others.

Part IV: DONATE

Chapter 9: Generosity

A Money Ninja understands that true wealth isn't just about how much you have, it's about how much you give. Generosity builds strong communities, creates opportunities, and brings happiness. A Money Ninja donates wisely, supports causes they care about, and gives their time, money, or skills to help others.

Part V: Conclusion to Money Ninja

Chapter 10: Protect Your Money Like a Ninja

Keeping money safe is just as important as making it. A Money Ninja guards their wealth by protecting their bank accounts, avoiding scams, using strong passwords, and setting up financial safety nets like insurance and emergency funds.

Chapter 11: Money Pitfalls Ninjas Can Avoid

Even the best Money Ninjas make mistakes, but they learn from them. Common money pitfalls include impulse spending, not saving early, ignoring budgets, and misusing credit. A Money Ninja reflects, adjusts, and stays focused on long-term success.

Your Next Steps as a Money Ninja

Now that you've completed this journey, it's time to take action. Here's how to continue applying what you've learned:

1. Set Your Financial Goals – Write down what you want to achieve in the next year and break it into smaller steps.
2. Create a Vision Board – Keep your money goals visible so you stay motivated.
3. Stick to Your Money Ninja Habits – Keep saving, investing, and learning about financial success.
4. Avoid Money Mistakes – Stay disciplined, use credit wisely, and always think before making financial decisions.
5. Keep Learning – The best Money Ninjas never stop improving. Read financial books, follow smart money habits, and continue growing your knowledge.

A Money Ninja takes control of their financial future. The choices you make today will shape the opportunities you have tomorrow. Whether you want financial freedom, a thriving business, or the ability to help others, it all starts with smart money decisions.

Your money journey doesn't end here, it's just beginning. Keep practicing, stay disciplined, and continue leveling up your financial skills. Your future self will thank you for becoming a Money Ninja today!

Expert Advice

"Dreams don't work unless you do." — John C. Maxwell

Having a vision is important, but it's your daily actions, saving, setting goals, and learning, that turn dreams into reality. A Money Ninja doesn't just wish for a better future, they plan for it.

Actionable Strategies

- Set one financial goal this week – Start small and build momentum.
- Make a mini vision board – Even a simple list of goals can keep you motivated.
- Track your progress – Keep a notebook or use an app to measure success.

"**The** best way to predict the future is to create it."
– PETER DRUCKER

Personal Story: How I Reached My First Money Goal

When I was younger, I wanted a gaming console. Instead of asking for money, I set a savings goal and created a plan. I babysat, saved birthday money, and skipped small purchases to reach my goal. A few months later, I had enough to buy it, and the feeling of accomplishing my goal was even better than the console itself! That's when I realized that financial planning isn't just about money, it's about proving to yourself that you can achieve anything with the right mindset and effort.

Quick Quiz Box

True or False:

1. Setting financial goals helps you stay motivated.
2. A vision board can help keep you focused on your money goals.
3. Planning your finances doesn't matter when you're young.

(Answers: T, T, F)

Journal Reflection Box

What is one big financial goal you have for the future? How will you start working toward it today?

YOUR MONEY FUTURE

Action Challenge Chart – Your Money Future

Task	Goal	Outcome
Set a 1-month money goal	Practice short-term planning	Build confidence in your money habits
Make a vision board (physical or digital)	Visualize your financial future	Stay inspired and focused
Open or explore a savings/investment account	Take action toward real-world goals	Become financially proactive
Write a letter to your future self	Imagine who you want to become	Set a mindset for long-term success

Mini-FAQ

Q1: What if I don't know what I want my future to look like yet?
A: That's okay! The goal isn't to have it all figured out, it's to start practicing habits that give you more options later. Saving, learning, and setting goals are all future-friendly moves.

Q2: How do I stay motivated to reach big goals?
A: Break them into smaller steps! Make a vision board or money tracker. Every dollar saved is a step forward, and small wins lead to big results.

Q3: What's the most powerful thing I can do for my future right now?
A: Believe in yourself. Start early. Stay consistent. Your future isn't something that just happens, it's something you build, one choice at a time.

Money Ninja Takeaway:

Your money journey starts now.
Dream it, plan it, do it.

FINAL THOUGHTS

YOUR JOURNEY TO FINANCIAL FREEDOM

A Note from Me to You

Throughout this journey, you've learned how to think like a Money Ninja, how to earn, save, invest, and protect your wealth, and how to build a strong financial future. But beyond the numbers, strategies, and exercises, there's something even more important, emotional strength.

Money is not just about numbers in a bank account. It's about confidence, choices, freedom, and security. It's about having the ability to take care of yourself, help others, and build a life that reflects your values and dreams. It's about becoming someone who isn't controlled by money but controls money wisely.

This journey is not about perfection, it's about progress. You might make mistakes, face setbacks, or feel like you're not moving fast enough. That's okay. Every mistake is a lesson, every challenge is an opportunity, and every small step forward is still progress.

Being a Money Ninja isn't just about financial skills, it's about resilience, patience, and discipline. It's about knowing that your future is in your hands, and you have the power to shape it, improve it, and make it something incredible.

So as you move forward, remember:

You are in control of your financial future. Every decision you make today shapes what's possible for you tomorrow.

Money is a tool, not a goal. Use it wisely to create opportunities, security, and freedom, not just to accumulate things.

Your journey will evolve. You will grow, your goals will change, and your financial knowledge will expand. Keep learning, keep improving, and stay curious.

Most of all, know that you already have everything you need to be financially strong. You have the ability to earn, save, invest, and give in a way that creates a life of meaning and fulfillment. You are on the right path, and this is just the beginning.

Thank you for taking this journey with me. Now, go forward with confidence, wisdom, and the heart of a true Money Ninja.

You've got this!

MONEY NINJA GLOSSARY

Asset – Something you own that has value and can grow over time, such as a house, stocks, or a business.

Budget – A plan for how you will spend and save your money.

Credit Score – A number that shows how trustworthy you are with borrowing money. A high score helps you qualify for loans with better interest rates.

Debt – Money you borrow and must pay back, often with interest.
Emergency Fund – Savings set aside for unexpected expenses, such as medical bills, car repairs, or job loss.

Expense – Money you spend on things, such as rent, food, clothes, and entertainment.

Income – Money you earn from jobs, businesses, or investments.

Interest – The cost of borrowing money or the money earned from savings/investments.

Investing – Using money to buy assets that can grow in value over time, such as stocks, real estate, or businesses.

Liability – A financial obligation or debt that you owe, such as a loan, credit card balance, or mortgage.

Net Worth – The total value of what you own (assets) minus what you owe (liabilities).

Passive Income – Money earned with little or no daily effort, such as rental income, stock dividends, or royalties.

Risk Tolerance – How comfortable you are with losing money in investments. Higher risk can lead to higher rewards, but also higher losses.

Savings Rate – The percentage of your income that you save rather than spend.

Stocks – A piece of ownership in a company that can grow in value over time and may pay dividends.

Tax-Advantaged Account – A savings or investment account that offers tax benefits, such as a Roth IRA or 401(k).

Wealth – The total value of your money, investments, and assets.

A Money Ninja stays informed, keeps learning, and applies these concepts daily to build a strong financial future.

MONEY NINJA CHALLENGES
(ACTIVITIES TO BUILD FINANCIAL CONFIDENCE)

Challenge 1: The No-Spend Challenge

- Go one week without spending money on non-essentials.
- Track what you would have spent and put that amount into savings.

Challenge 2: The $10 Savings Challenge

- Save $10 this week by skipping one unnecessary purchase.
- Repeat for a month and see how much you've saved!

Challenge 3: The 24-Hour Rule

- Before buying anything over $20, wait 24 hours.
- If you still want it after a day, go for it. If not, save your money!

Challenge 4: Create a Vision Board

- Find pictures and words that represent your financial goals.
- Keep your board somewhere visible as a daily reminder.

Challenge 5: Track Every Dollar for One Week

- Write down everything you spend for seven days.
- At the end of the week, see where you can cut back and save more.

Challenge 6: Open a Savings Account

- If you don't already have one, ask a parent or guardian about opening a savings account.
- Deposit at least $20 and watch your money grow!

Challenge 7: Research an Investment

- Choose one stock, mutual fund, or real estate investment to research.
- Write down what you learn and see if it's something you'd consider investing in one day.

Challenge 8: Find a Side Hustle

- Brainstorm three ways you could earn extra money.
- Pick one and try it out for a week!

Challenge 9: Give Back

- Donate a small amount to a cause you care about or volunteer for an hour.
- Reflect on how giving makes an impact beyond money.

Challenge 10: Set a Money Goal

- Write down one financial goal for the next 30 days.
- Create an action plan to reach it and track your progress.

Earnings Exercises: Boost Your Income Skills

Exercise 1: Identify Your Money-Making Strengths

- Write down three things you're good at (e.g., tutoring, graphic design, coding, organizing).
- Research how people make money with those skills (side hustles, part-time jobs, freelance work).
- Choose one skill and create a simple plan to start earning (like selling a service, babysitting, or flipping items online).

Exercise 2: Money Ninja Side Hustle Challenge

- Pick one small way to earn extra money this month.
- Examples: Sell old clothes online, offer a service, tutor a younger student, or create digital products.
- Set a goal to earn at least $20 in the next two weeks.

Exercise 3: Track How Much You Make

- Keep a log of every dollar you earn this month.
- Write down where the money came from (job, gifts, side hustle).
- Analyze which income streams work best and plan ways to increase them.

Savings Exercises: Build Your Money Fortress

Exercise 4: The 24-Hour Spending Rule

- The next time you want to buy something non-essential, wait 24 hours before purchasing.
- Ask yourself: Do I still want it? Can I find it cheaper? Is it worth it?
- If you no longer feel like buying it, put that money into savings instead.

Exercise 5: The $5 Savings Challenge

- Every time you receive a $5 bill, save it instead of spending it.
- Set a goal (e.g., save $50 in $5 bills by the end of the month).
- Count how much you've saved after 30 days!

Exercise 6: Automate Your Savings

- If you don't already, set up an automatic transfer from your checking account to a savings account.
- Even if it's $5 or $10 a week, make saving effortless.
- After a month, check your progress and increase your savings amount if possible.

Investments Exercises: Make Your Money Work for You

Exercise 7: Learn the Magic of Compound Interest

- Use a compound interest calculator (like Investor.gov) to see how much money grows over time.
- Enter different amounts ($100, $500, or $1,000) and see how much it grows with 5% or 10% interest over 10+ years.
- Write down why starting early is important based on what you learned.

Exercise 8: Research One Investment Option

- Pick one investment type (stocks, index funds, real estate, crypto).
- Research how it works, the risks, and how people make money with it.
- Write three key takeaways you learned about investing.

Exercise 9: Follow the Stock Market for a Week

- Choose three companies you like (Nike, Apple, Disney, etc.).
- Check their stock prices daily for a week.

- Write down how much they go up or down, and learn what affects stock prices.

Generosity Exercises: Give with Purpose

Exercise 10: Random Acts of Financial Kindness

- Do one generous act with money this week. Ideas:
  » Buy coffee for a friend.
  » Donate $5 to a charity.
  » Pay for someone's lunch.
- Notice how it makes you feel and how it impacts someone else.

Exercise 11: Research a Cause You Care About

- Pick a cause (education, the environment, animal rescue, hunger relief).
- Find one nonprofit organization working on that cause.
- Learn how you can support them financially or through volunteering.

Exercise 12: Give Without Spending Money

- Find a way to give back without donating money:
  » Volunteer at an event.
  » Help a neighbor with chores.
  » Tutor someone for free.
- Write about how generosity isn't just about money, it's about impact.

Protect Your Money Ninja Exercises: Guard Your Wealth

Exercise 13: Strengthen Your Financial Security

- Update all passwords for your online banking and financial accounts.

- Enable two-factor authentication (2FA) for extra security.
- Check your bank statements for any unexpected transactions.

Exercise 14: Spot a Scam

- Research common financial scams (phishing emails, fake lottery winnings, IRS scams).
- Find an example online (news articles or scam reports).
- Write down three ways to spot a scam and how to protect yourself.

Exercise 15: Start Your Emergency Fund

- If you don't already have one, open a separate savings account for emergencies.
- Deposit at least $10 this week into the fund.
- Set a goal to reach $100, then $500, then $1,000.

Ultimate Money Ninja Challenge: Create Your Money Ninja Plan

Step 1: Set Your Top 3 Money Goals

- Write down three specific, realistic, and measurable financial goals.

Step 2: Make an Action Plan

- Break down each goal into small steps (daily, weekly, monthly).

Step 3: Track Your Progress

- Use a journal, spreadsheet, or app to track your savings, income, and investments.

Step 4: Review & Adjust

- Every 30 days, check your progress. If something isn't working, adjust your plan and keep moving forward.

Being a Money Ninja is a lifelong journey. These exercises help build strong money habits, but the key to success is consistency. Keep setting goals, learning about money, and improving your financial skills.

Remember:

Small habits lead to big results.

Mistakes are lessons, learn and keep going!

Your future self will thank you for starting today.

Now go out there and train like a true Money Ninja!

MONEY NINJA CHALLENGES

Other Products by Mary Nhin

 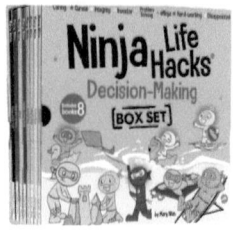 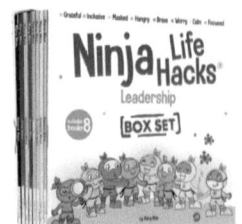
 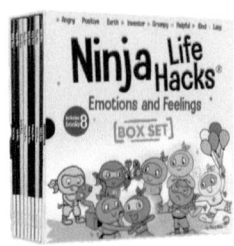 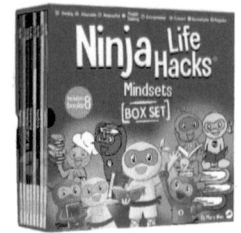

NinjaLifeHacks.tv

About the Author

Mary Nhin is a social impact entrepreneur and author of the flagship series, Ninja Life Hacks, a social-emotional learning brand, with 124 books and 99 characters, dedicated to empowering children with life skills. It's captured the hearts of over four million readers and continues to lead the way for an exciting adventure in social, emotional learning.

At the core of Mary Nhin's writing is a flicker of hope. While the writer frequently lays her soul bare, tackling issues such as failures, acceptance, and loneliness, there's always a silver lining. That's particularly true of her book series, "Ninja Life Hacks," which looks at failures as a transformative experience.

Under Mary's leadership, the Ninja Life Hacks brand of books, resources, and toys have empowered people worldwide with social, emotional coping strategies to use for a lifetime. Her books have been translated in twelve countries.

As Co-founder and Chief Creative Officer of Nhinja Sushi, the mom and pop restaurant has blossomed into a five location restaurant chain, serving up high quality sushi and freshly cooked meals to busy families. Today, over 1500+ people visit Nhinja locations daily.

Mary's visionary leadership earned her and her teams a collection of industry accolades including: Woman of Integrity Award Winner (Better Business Bureau), Most Admired CEO (The Journal Record), HER award (405 Magazine), Top 50 Most Influential Oklahomans Power List (Journal Record), Top 100

Small Businesses (U.S. Chamber of Commerce), AAPI Strong Restaurant Winner (National ACE), In the Lead Female Leader (Journal Record), 40 Under Forty (OKC Business), Inc 5000 (Inc. Magazine), Best Sushi (Edmond Life and Leisure and Edmond Sun), Best Finance Books For Kids (Investopedia), Best Kids Money Books (Mom.com).

    She and her husband, Kang Nhin, are proud parents of three children, Mikey, Kobe, and Jojo.

WEBSITE: www.ninjalifehacks.tv

WEBSITE: www.nhinja.com

LINKEDIN: @Marynhin

FB: Nhinja Sushi

FB: Ninja Life Hacks

IG: @nhinjasushi

IG: @officialninjalifehacks

TT: @officialninjalifehacks

YT: youtube.com/@NinjaLifeHacks

X: @nhinjas

Email: mary@ninjalifehacks.tv

www.ingramcontent.com/pod-product-compliance
Ingram Content Group UK Ltd.
Pitfield, Milton Keynes, MK11 3LW, UK
UKHW042004230426
12048UKWH00009B/547